EUROPE
AND AMERICA

Published under the auspices of
the Danish Bicentennial Committee to commemorate
the 200th Anniversary of the American Revolution.

1976

C. F. von Schmidt-Phiseldek
EUROPE AND AMERICA

Facsimile edition

THE ROYAL DANISH MINISTRY OF FOREIGN AFFAIRS
RHODOS, International Science and Art Publishers, Copenhagen

C. F. von Schmidt-Phiseldek: EUROPE AND AMERICA
Facsimile edition

© RHODOS, Copenhagen 1976
Lay-out by Michael Malling

Plates selected by Erik Alstrup
Postscript by Thorkild Kjærgaard .

The original edition of EUROPE AND AMERICA, published in 1820 and on which the present facsimile edition is based, had no illustrations. The publishers have, however, found it appropriate to provide the facsimile edition with illustrations culled from museums, art collections and libraries, notably the Royal Library in Copenhagen, but from collections in the United States as well. The purpose is to give the reader a visual impression as well of the period during which Schmidt-Phiseldek recorded his thoughts about Europe and America. Moreover a historian's postscript has been added, not only in order to put Schmidt-Phiseldek's book in the proper contemporary and present-day perspective but also to make it clear that Schmidt-Phiseldek was a man of considerable reputation at the time he wrote his famous book which today exists in a handful of copies only.

The book's sidepaper: Contemporary print from the collection of The Royal Danish Museum of Fine Arts.

Print: Bording Grafik A.S.
Binding: Th. Mortensen

ISBN 87 749 6532 8

Europe and America

or

the relative state of the civilized world at a future period.

———————

Translated from the German

of

Dr. C. F. von Schmidt-Phiseldek,

Doctor of philosophy, one of his Danish
Majesty's counsellors of state,
Knight of Dannebrog
&c, &c, &c.

by

Joseph Owen.

———————

Copenhagen 1820.
Printed by Bernhard Schlesinger.

Table of contents

*) In the English translation the author's last name is spelled Schmidt-Phiseldek. This spelling has been retained on the new title pages of the present edition. In all other places the common spelling of Schmidt-Phiseldeck has been used.

Introduction of the translator.

Animated with the desire of being the humble instrument of imparting to the American nation, that picture of future grandeur and happiness, which the author of the present interesting work, so prophetically holds out to them, I have been induced to undertake the translation of it. The diffidence I feel on the occasion, is considerably heightened by a fear, that the task I have imposed upon myself, has exceeded my abilities, and by a consciousness, of not having rendered justice, to the beauties of the original. A faithful adherence to the style of the author, where-ever the spirit of the two languages would admit of it, has been my ruling aim throughout the whole.

This work, which has met with the most favorable reception in Germany, has in the course of a few months, undergone a second edition, and has been translated into French and Danish, which amply vouch for its intrinsic merits. Could I flatter myself, that the present imperfect translation will engage the attention of the American public, I shall be fully rewarded, in having been the means of disseminating across the Atlantic those sublime and noble sentiments of the author, which do him honor as a philosopher, and a friend of humanity. With depth of penetration, deducing the events of Europe for the last forty years, from the establishment of Columbian independence, he portrays, with masterly hand, their awful and variegated course; points out those infirmities of the nations, which called down upon the present generation, the scenes of misery, it has experienced, and with the benevolent spirit of humanity paints in striking colours, the only means, by which, both princes and their people can steer aloof from future danger. The fate of Europe at a distant age, and the encreasing grandeur of America, now engage the author's thoughts, and plunging into futurity, he brings to light with daring hand, a picture, highly advantageous for the latter; but true to the principles, which shine so conspicuously throughout his work, consoles the former, for her loss of external political weight, with the prospect of internal happiness, and a fund of intellectual enjoyment.

Posterity will alone be able to judge of the correctness of our author's prophetic ideas; recent events speak in favour of them; it nevertheless redounds to his lasting honor, to have sketched out a future possible condition of the civilized world; to have illumined the steps of mankind, towards the summit of earthly perfection; and to have delivered his sentiments with that independent freedom, which becomes the enlightened age we live in, and which thrives so luxuriantly in the congenial soil of America.

Contents.

the dominion of the world; on the other hand,
America, has no need of any of the European
natural productions, and will shortly be able
to do without her artificial productions. Great
advantages of America, with regard to her
means of internal communications; probability that America will also attain mercantile
independence.

IX. How could Europe be indemnified for the loss
of America? If she will retain and extend
her other commercial channels, and be able
to open new ones for her productions and fa-
brications; grounds against this; failure or at
least great decrease of the customary supplies
of gold and silver; on this the trade to China
and Japan must cease, and fall into the hands
of the Americans; uncertain state of things
in British India; apprehension of political
changes there; the flourishing increase of the
American East-India trade; increasing American carrying-trade; her navy and commercial shipping must shortly, according to all
natural consequences, become the most powerful and numerous; America much better
suited for intercourse, with the present European possessions and establishments in Africa
and the South-Sea; neither will she be deficient in European intelligence; conclusive
result of this.

X. Europe, by withdrawing within herself, by internal cultivation, and by extending her nearest confines, must replace her external losses.
The idea of one European political community
must be called into life; then Europe will be
powerful, and be able to supply her own wants,
without transmarine possessions; what mischief

Preface.

That mind which has elevated itself to a state of self-activity, from amidst the pressure of the established state of human affairs, will above all strive, so to exalt itself, as to have an open and unbiassed view of the wordly system of things, in order to be able to distinguish from thence, as from a lofty eminence, its own proper place in the mighty whole, and to survey the course of those events, with which it discovers itself to be interwoven.

But this world can only be viewed in a twofold light: through the principles of experience, or through those of idea; the former could also be

termed the view of the digestive, the latter of the
creative understanding or inward intuition. —

These points of view, are, according to their
direction, entirely separated. The observer from
the one, considers the world as a given whole,
which, as soon as it received the first impulse, began
unfolding itself, by the thread of the laws of nature,
founded on causes and effects, in one infinite succession; every thing will happen, which can happen, and the way in which it comes to pass, is the
only one, in which it can and must take place, for
nothing new occurs under the sun, every thing appearing and disappearing, in order eternally to be
repeated, and reproduced. From the other point
of view, the wise man contemplates the world, according to laws, which reason prescribes for a
world, destined to attain its sublimest ends. The
one regards the world, as it appears to the sensual
eye, the other constructs it, at it should be, according to the dictates of reason, realized by experience. —

The great question, which will be liable to be
decided by minds of superior intellectual powers,
but not long before the close of the history of the

human race, is this: are both these views of the world to be amalgamated, or are they to be eternally separated, and directly opposed to each other? does the world as it is, contain within itself, the ideal world as embryo, and do the laws of experience become gradually subordinate, and at last lose themselves in idea, or does the material world, eternally opposed to the latter, constitute a region of its own, obliging idea to take refuge in a future world, the offspring only of its fondest wishes? —

Without wishing to anticipate either the metaphysician or the historian, the unbiassed contemplation of the occurrences of the world must lead to the conclusion, that the mere laws of nature, and their constant and infinite developement from primitive causes, are by no means sufficient to explain them, in an intelligent manner, deserving the estimation, they are worthy of; — but we must allow the human mind the Liberty, that is the faculty of absolutely connecting afresh, a string of causes and effects, which being interwoven, fit decidedly in the principal connection of things, without, as far as enquiry reaches, being controuled by it. —

(1*)

In other words: the living generation of mankind, does not always suffer itself, just to go the
road, the pressure of necessity may force or lead it;
from time to time a spark of light flashes forth, not
kindled in this world; loftiness of soul resists, and
paves its way to those points, which diametrically
oppose every pressure of circumstances, and disgrace
every common calculation of the course of human
affairs. These lucid points of history form the boundaries of an old, and a new age. The powerful spirits, which uncontrouled, and free from earthly
eye, bring down to mortals the celestial fire, uniting the invisible, with the visible and perishable
world, hurry along with them, their more feeble
cotemporaries, and from the matter deposited by
them, as an eternal fund for future ages to work
upon, a fresh fermentation arises, affording the understanding, capable of digesting it, for a length of
time nourishment and occupation. —

Thus lived and acted the great men and heroes
of every age; and that which is good and beautiful in
this world, is nothing but the exposition of certain
sublime and lofty thoughts, which appear originally
not to have belonged to it.

Our age has also witnessed great events, and the coldness of our understanding, ever dismembering and disuniting, and which dissolved the animated world at last into an empty, hollow nothing, is, by an universal inspiration, once more penetrated through and through by light and warmth. — Called away, by oppression from mere abstractions, to take part in the actions, and sufferings of civil society, we find ourselves placed at a barrier, which irrevocably separates what is Old, from the New which is yet to come; light and oetherial warmth hover over a mass in a state of fermentation, which must first settle and be at rest, before the union of both, will remodel the form of civil and political life. —

On the point of a revolution of this nature taking place, be it allowed to pause, in order to draw off and exhibit to the understanding, which on no account suffers its occupation to be wrested forcibly from it, what is liable to be developed from the given impulse and elements at hand, addressing at the same time, a few words of admonition and moderation to the cotemporaries of this age, so manifoldly agitated.

In like manner, as spirits come not in immediate contact with each other, carrying on their intercourse through the vehicle of the thoughts, which as a moveable power adjust and order spiritual life, — so does all the intercourse of material life, depend and rest upon Money, itself the offspring of the brightest imagination, penetrating and comprehending all the various relations of the outward world. — But the Outward being a reflection of the Inward, every new impulse from the intellectual world, must determine and remodel outward life, and the effects of its springs of action; but the very nature of the things it meets with in the material world, prescribes bounds to its operation. —

The later times have witnessed this world held together, governed, and tyrannised by money, and a system of calculation in the most extended sense of the word, all the animated powers and the measure of their exertions, being only rated according to numbers; the world's greatest gamesters were under the influence of numbers, and grounded their plans on a calculation, which tore up by the roots all the self-dependance and dignity of the individual. But a nobler inspiration has burst this chain asunder; that, has happened, which no calculator, could have supposed possible, from the exhausted pecuniary resources, and disposeable physical powers of the several nations, according to the usual suppositions; and the most pleasing result of enormous exertions, is, that the individual is again admitted to be more, and something else, than its numerical unity. —

The revolution from old to new times, has ever been a period attended with pressure and affliction to the human race, in which the stronger have to contend with prodigious difficulties under the weight of which, many must sink, ere the goal be reached, but the weaker, — who are always the more numerous — must go to ruin under sufferings and privations of every description. — Although unavoidable upon the whole, this fate can be alleviated, by intelligent and enlightened attention being paid to the character of the times, and instead of opposing its spirit — by meeting it, and directing the wild tendency of individuals towards that side where the great mass of the people irresistably inclines. In like manner, as the period just past away, or in the act of taking leave of us, was subject to the principles of mechanism and pecuniary calculations, so, can it be expected, that money, for the time to come, will of necessity, be subordinate to a more exalted animated power. — To shew, in what manner this change will be liable to happen, and the results it may produce, with regard to a new formation of the civil state of things, — is the object of the following considerations, which we offer, not, as a positive acknowledgment of facts, but to rouse the attention, stimulate to deeper enquiry, and to lead to more enlightened instruction.

I.

The fourth of July, in the Year 1776 points out the commencement of a new period in the history of the world. — Not provoked to resistance, by the intolerable oppression of tyrannical power, but imbittered by the arbitray encroachments upon well earned, and hitherto publicly acknowledged privileges, the people of the United States of North-America, declared themselves on that memorable day, independant of the dominion of the British Islands, generally speaking mild and benevolent in itself, and under which they had hitherto stood, as a colony, in a state, not of slavish servitude, but of partial guardianship, under the protection of the mother country.

England, who disdained to stand upon a footing of equality with its former wards and to resign the guardianship, it had so long maintained, prolonged the conflict, as long as any hopes of success remained, and drew the rest of Europe into the

domestic quarrel, either for or against the cause of
independance. The spark that had once been kindled,
being by these means carried to this side of the
ocean, readily met with combustible materials here,
and a spirit of enquiry into the rights of man, and
a struggling after a lawful independance, consequently after forms of government, which should be
able to protect the individual, against the arbitrary
hand of power, had from the other side, laid hold
of the more enlightened heads; and the commencement of the French fermentations, which more or
less electrified all Europe, followed almost immediately upon the peace of Paris (the 20th Jany.
1783), which associated North-America as an independant state, with the ancient body of nations. —

The newly-formed Republic constituted itself *) on principles which promised the confederacy
enlargement and consistency, not derived from
the conquest of subject provinces, but from the
junction of new States, which must shortly arise
in its extensive territories under the influence of an
encreasing population. This result happened earlier, and upon a much larger scale, than the most
sanguine expectations could have prognosticated, and
America proved very soon, that she was not alone

---

*) By the act of Constitution of the United States of
North-America of the 17 Sep, 1787.

capable of existing as a state, but that she meant to
take an active part in the affairs of the world, the
discussion and arrangement of which, had hitherto
been left to the nations of Europe; by which she
was aiming a blow at the general system of European politics. As early as 1803, she displayed her
standard in the Mediterranean, chastizing the piryat-
ical state of Tripolis, and twenty years after the
foundation of a solid constitution *), the jealousy
of Great Britain kindled the first hostile spark,
which being once more stirred up from the ashes, by
the attack made on the English Sloop of war, the
Little Belt **) burst out into open flames, which
were only extinguished three years later, by the
peace of Ghent ***).

By these occurrences, which we have here only
cursorily touched upon, the North-American independant state, had tried her strength, preserved her
dignity, by the rejection of illegal pretensions, and
vigorously proved and maintained her right, as an
active member in the scale of nations, to take part
in the grand affairs of the civilized world. From
that moment the impulse towards a new change of

---

*) Attack of the British on the Chesapeake frigate
the 20 July 1807.
**) The 16 May 1811.
***) 24 Dec. 1814.

events, ceased to proceed exclusively from the old
continent, and it is possible, that in a short time it
will emanate wholly from the new one. For its
southern part had by no means been an idle spectator of the recent changes under the northern
hemisphere; the success they were attended with,
had raised also hopes there, and developed claims,
which must lead to similar results. Under the dominion of the mother-country, the Spanish colonies
to the North and South of the Isthmus of Darien,
could only flourish slowly and sparingly; but they
were nevertheless in an improving state, and it was
by no means the yoke of an intolerable despotism,
that despair had endeavored to shake of. The
Spanish government, had time after time extended
the oppressive commercial monopoly *); opulence
and luxury reigned in the larger cities, and even
the rigour of slavery was mitigated by more benevolent laws. But the collision of the different
castes, of which the natives of mixed races viewed
with jealous eye, the privileges of the born Spaniard;
the awakened instinct of wishing to have a self-de-
termining voice in the affairs of their own country;
the want of prudence in the existing government,

---

*) To be seen on this subject in: Tableau de
l'Espagne moderne par J. T. r. Bourgoing 4me
Edition à Paris 1807, Tom. II pag. 188. sq.

unwieldy and slow in all the forms of its administrative justice, in not meeting this rising spirit;
but above all, the glorious example of North-America
called forth the first attempts at Emancipation.

This word as intimating the resistance of a
people, feeling themselvss at maturity, against their
wonted tutelage, and desirous of taking upon themselves the management of their own affairs, most
suitably expresses that spirit of the times, which
being called to light in 1776 has spread itself over
the new and old world. — These attempts at emancipation, have in a short space of time, been followed by an almost universal revolt in South
America. —

As early as 1806, the daring Don Francesco
Miranda, had endeavoured to deliver his country
from the dominion of Spain, without finding at
that time participation and support sufficient, to
withstand superior force. In the mean time, the
seed which had been sown, did not remain unfruitful.
The revolution which took place later in the mother-
country, gave the thirst after innovation, the wished
for pretext, and at least a very plausible air of
legality. The imprudent conduct of the Central
Junta, who represented the resigned Dynasty, and
the impossibility of a vigorous cooperation on the
part of the nominal ruler of Spain and the Indies,
but whose power in fact extended no farther than

Madrid and its neigborhood, completed the explosion. The cotemporary emigration of the Portuguese government from Europe to the Brazils towards the close of 1807, which seated perhaps unknown to it on a vulcano, was already inclined towards the extension rather than the strengthning of this beautiful kingdom, may be assigned as an incident promoting the general insurrection.

In the course of the year 1810, Caraccas, Quito, la Plata and Mexico reared the standard of independance, and received Miranda in triumph at Guaira, who returned the following year, to devote himself afresh to a conflict, in which he fell, it is true, but without ruining the cause he fought for. The legitimate government, which was restored on the 19 March 1814, found matters too far gone, and the resources of the kingdom too much exhausted, as also too much occupation and too many disturbances in the mother - country, to be able to put a sufficient barrier to the progress of the revolutionary colonies: —

According to the public acknowledged state of affairs, we may draw this decisive conclusion, that although Spain, may be fortunate enough to retain her West India islands under her ancient dominion, the South-American continent, will sooner or later withdraw itself from it, and that at least, several large independant states will join the national

confederacy of the civilized world. It is to be
supposed, that the similitude of the constitutional
forms, and an equal interest against the attempts
of European powers, will unite these new states in
a close compact, wtth the North - American confederacy; and if a quarter of a century only elapsed,
before North- America began to act externally with
vigor, it may be presumed, that the younger states
of the Southern continent, endowed with more
ample resources, and a more ancient culture, will
require a shorter period, to arrive at a state of
respectable force. — It is suitable to the human
spirit of enquiry, and is not likely to be a useless
undertaking, to cast a prying look into futurity,
and generally to sketch the outlines of the new form
of the civilized world, according to the results,
which the intimated spirit of the times is likely to
produce. — But as the understanding in all its
operations, is confined to the matter that is laid
before it, and can only develope future forms by
making use of the existing ones, a description of the
situation of the civilized world on its entrance into
the new change of things, must precede the representation we have in question, if an enquiry of this
nature is not to degenerate into an empty flight of
the imagination.

II.

The new spirit that had been called to life on the other side of the Atlantic, and the universal fermentation it caused, happened at a period, in which the most excessive laxness reigned predominant on the old continent. The political existence of the people was for the most part extinguished; their active industry had been directed abroad, and the governments, finding no opposition or dangerous collisions, internally, followed with the stream. Commerce, exportations, colonial systems, every means of acquiring money, were cherished and protected, riches presenting the only possibility, of investing the low with consideration and influence, and the high, with power and inordinate dominion. — The maxims, according to which the nations were governed, laid less in the ground-pillars of an existing constitution, than in the changeable systems of the cabinets, and the nature of their rulers; there remained for the most part, nothing for the great body of the people, but to be spectators. —

Germany, the grand heart of Europe, presented now, nothing more, than the shadow of a political body united in one common confederacy; the imperial government, as also the administration of the federal-laws, were without energy, and

united efforts to repel invasions from abroad, had
not been witnessed, since the danger threatened by
the Turks, had ceased. The larger states', grown
out of their obedience, were often ranged in alliance
against the Head, which was scarcely capable itself
of protecting the weaker, against injuries. — The
mighty contention, between the old and new church,
had long been thrown aside; religion had lost its
political interest, and had already passed the boundaries of rational toleration, and had reached the
extreme of a perfect indifference to all interests which
did not immediately concern physical well-being;
the people, however, had preserved a more religious
feeling, and purer morals upon the whole, than
were to be expected from the tenets of the age. —

The internal affairs of the individual vassal
states, were exclusively conducted, according to the
will of their regents; the energy and the importance
of the representative popular estates, were become
dormant, and the standing armies, which had been
introduced by degrees even into the smallest prin-
cipalities, since the peace of Westphalia, being
perfectly foreign to the hearts and dispositions of
the people, threw an astonishing weight into the
scale of unlimited sovereignty. Being mercenary
combatants, (soldiers) recruted from every nation,
modelled upon a system of blind subordination, and

raised by Frederick in Prussia, (who only in that age, could, through them, be termed the Great,) to the highest pitch of perfection, they had been accomplices in diffusing this system of despotism over all the different relations of the state, and in leaving the people, who were freed from military exercise, nothing but the acquirement of gain. Agriculture, agreable to the direction given it, had been improved, and with it population encreased; industry, supported by the progress of the mechanical arts, had been considerably extended, and governments upon the whole just, and mild in themselves, had, it cannot be denied, tolerably well taken care of the physical welfare of the subject. The civil administrations, delivered from internal opposition, fostered, in unison with individual exertions, the several branches of emolument, in order to provide for money, as the means of aggrandizement; they farmed each their greater or lesser territory, according to its population and productions, as the feodal proprietor does his land, in order to bring forth the greatest possible financial result. But as each government did this after its own manner, viewing its neighbour with a jealous eye, the whole of Germany never reaped any beneficial result from it, and all the various institutions inimically directed against each other, were reared on loose foundations, and must fall together on the

first externed shock. — Circumstances like these
were incapable of producing an universal national
character. — There, where no reciprocal tie binds
the individuals of a state together, who living under
the equal laws of one community, ought to form
one solid whole, the spirit of the nation loses itself
in different directions, and the attainment of individual welfare many be gained, but never will a
true sense of what is Great, and universally Good,
be promoted. It can plainly be seen, that the German learned constitution, not having the foundation
of a political existence, in which it could have
found consistency, and which is could so well have
employed, floated as a mere airy bubble between
heaven and earth. Imagination, in which the
German, above all others, displays so great a ferti-
lity, wanted a medium, in which it could prove the
validity of its representations; which not finding,
it lost itself in the wide field of doubt, and took refuge in subtile abstractions. Actual knowledge was
become the property of a peculiar class of men,
who amusing, blaming, and admiring each other,
threw back their light principally on themselves,
and seldom had any real influence on the people. —
The arts of oratory, so highly cultivated by the
ancients, were sunk down to bookish arts, and those
of the more plastic kind, were either kept at a
distance under the veil of a mythology, wholly

foreign and unintelligible to the people, or were content with the slender nourishment, the deviation from the simplicity of a religion entirely spiritual, afforded them. Only those branches of human knowledge, such as mathematics, chymistry with their attendant sciences, which are directed towards the investigation of nature, and the utility of its different properties, had penetrated so far, as to be immediately applied to the purposes of common life; and by the side of these, flourished those acquirements, which are founded on skill and experience, and such as render the encrease of capital more easy, by facilitating the exchange of the various productions of the earth, from pole to pole. —

If in Germany, where the imperial crown represented a mere shadow, deprived of power and consequence, the mighty vassals were all, — in France the crown was every thing, after it had victoriously subdued the powerful Barons and other nobles of the country; and the people represented indeed as a nation one body, but were deprived, like the several German states, of all political weight, and were arbitrarily subjected to every impulse of the government *). The same was the case in

---

*) The appearance of a constitutional opposition, which the Parlementarians wished to give themselves, was in fact, according to historical

Conrad Georg Friedrich Elias von Schmidt-Phiseldeck (1770–1832)

Norwegian iron works, c. 1790

Spain and Portugal, where religious intolera-
tion more powerfully suppressed every utterance of
contrary opinions, and every doctrine which might
lead to the deviation from the maxims of the state,
so intimately connected with those of the priesthood.
Although, since the violent revocation of the edict
of Nantes, an outward appearance of unity in religion, and its public worship, reigned in France,
yet, a tolerably wide undisturbed field was left to
opinions, differing from those of the established
church, provided they did not shew themselves in
any conspicuous way. On the other hand, the more
serious and profound character of the former nations,
held the tie much closer together, between the rulers
and the people, attached to the throne by religion,
and by a far more rigid adherence to customs and
maxims frought with veneration, than on this side
of the Pyrennees, where frivolity irreverently trifled
with every thing that was holy, and novelty lent a
charm to every dazzling chimera, which tended towards daring attempts at political reforms, substituted one after the other, by the designs of unruly
heads.

---

sources, an usurpation, the motives of which,
laid more in court-cabals, than in any interest
they took in the fate of the people.

The tendency of the governments in Germany, being directed towards the aggrandizemement of their territories, at the expence of the confederate states and a complete dislocation of the surrounding weak national edifice; the states which were completely consolidated under the sovereign power of the crown, must naturally direct their ambitious aims at their foreign neighbours. In such manner were France and Spain leagued against the commercial and colonial-interets, and not less against the industry and encreasing naval power of Great Britain, whilst Portugal, chained, since Methuens celebrated treaty *), to the monopoly of England, from which it had vainly endeavored to free itself, under Pombals administration, was nearly sunk into the condition of a British colony, working its gold mines in the Brazils, for the benefit of the proud islanders.

Italy parcelled out amongst different powers, presented upon the whole, the same political appearance as Germany, only with the difference of its being totally void of the shadow of unity, which the latter appeared at least to possess under the Imperial sceptre. Upper and a great part of middle

---

*) Closed under Peter the second of Portugal and Queen Ann of England 1702.

Italy being totally dismembered, were subservient
to foreign impulse; the lower part, with the fertile
island on the other side of the Pharus, presented,
to be sure, since 1735, the outward appearance of
one national whole, but was too weak to withstand
the fate of the more powerful Bourbon-families,
from which according to treaties it had derived its
sovereigns. There reigned in the Papal state alone,
which could not derive its weight from its worldly
sovereignty, but from the spiritual supremacy of its
ruler, the ancient maxims of the Romish pontificate
with the oeconomical state faults of clerical government. But the consideration and the power of the
former were visibly sunken; the journeys of the
Pope of that time, to Vienna, were, like the cotemporary ones *), of the Hierarch of Thibet to
China, rather prejudicial than favorable to spiritual
influence and dignity; the faulty internal administration of the state seemed to court every attempt
at innovation. — The republics to the East and
West of the Adriatic Gulph, were, since the flourishing rise of the great naval states, only the
ruins of past glory, sinking visibly daily, into in-
significance. Notwithstanding, neither was the

---

*) See on this subject: Ambassade au Thibet et
   au Boutan par Mr. Tourner; traduit de l'An-
   glais par Castéra; II Tomes à Paris 1800.

image of former greatness blotted from the memo-
ries, nor a proper feeling for it extinguished in the
minds of the inhabitants of the luxuriant peninsula; the pride of the more noble fed itself on the
sublime remains of Roman antiquity; and the monuments of the golden age of the family of Medi-
cis, indemnified a people given to the arts, and full
of fire, for the loss of present grandeur, and kept
up in it, a lively presentement of a better futurity,
founded on the merits of its ancestors. —

Helvetia hemmed in, between Italy, Germany and France, by its mountains, continued in
the peaceable enjoyment of its liberty, through the
respect, its venerable age had universally diffused;
nevertheless, the disturbances at Geneva, and the
encreasing spirit of emigration, were sufficient to
shew, that a people who first begin to be indifferent to the present order of things, would willingly
have recourse to a system of innovation, as a suppo-
sitious antidote against many an arbitrary measure;
by which the ancient ties, which had held the happy
Swiss nation so many centuries together, became
slackened and relaxed. —

The dissolution of the existing form of government, in the North - Western Netherlands,
which ought never to have been separated from the
German corporation, was more visibly approaching;
the unwieldiness of their disorganized union, had

Alexander Hill Everett (1790–1847)

The Coal Waggon

no remedy to administer to the decline of their commerce and naval power, which became more and more felt, being a natural consequence of the daily encreasing concentration of the larger states; and it was evident, that the fate of the republic, would be decided by, and depended on a blow from abroad. —

The British-Islands, — at that time, the only country in Europe, which united under a monarchial head, moderate, but on that account, more solid principles of freedom, with a equal balance of the different powers of the state — were at the commencement of the American disturbances, in a progressive state of the most flourishing prosperity. For this happy condition, they were indebted to their freedom, and elegible commercial situation, together with the inexhaustible treasures, nature has deposited in their coal mines, on the existence of which, the industry of their diligent inhabitants is principally founded. Political ebullition, existed in no higher degree, than was necessary to give proper life and less perhaps, than was necessary to preserve in all its purity, a constitution, which long since acquired after the most bloody struggles was more deeply rooted in the mode of thinking, and in the manners and customs of the nation, than it was imprinted on them, by the letter of the law. The government had sufficient leisure to direct its

(4)

attention to abroad, and by means of hostile enterprizes and political treaties, which must sooner or
later give a naval power a most decided ascendancy,
held out a helping hand, to the commercial spirit
of the people, who aimed at making, (and with encreasing hopes of succes), the remainder of the
world tributary to it, for the productions of its fabrics and manufactories. — The plan, of supporting
commerce, upon territorial acquisitions, and of forming a kingdom out of the conquered provinces of
India, whose treasures should flow back to the
Queen of cities on the Thamse, was already fully
developed, and the exasperation against the Western
colonies, was to be attributed as much to a miscon-
strued commercial interest, as to a thirst of dominion; for these dared only to resist the principles
of taxation, but not to disavow the Supremacy of
the crown. The above named ingredients of the
British national character, ever more coldly repulsive — than aimiably attractive in its nature, had
produced an almost universal antipathy not alone
of the public mind, but also of the individual affections, against a people, in so many points of view,
so highly respectable, and being unceassingly fed
by that envy, which superiority involuntarily
creates, produced the most conspicuous influence
in the developement of the later events. —

In the East of Europe, the first division of Poland in 1772, had given the most unequivocal proof of the exclusive arbitrariness of the different cabinets, and of the formidable weight of standing armies. The system of political calculation, which rendered the interets of the people subservient to the abstractive idea of "State", and to the conveniences of such abstraction, was for the first time fully exposed to light; and the adoption of this system for twenty years, under which, this unfortunate kingdom suffered in the most convulsive agonies, until its political existence was at length formally annihilated by the last act of dismemberment, (the 24 October 1795) seemed to forebode its future extensive application.

It is unnecessary, to give a further exposition of the leading principles, which had possessed the three courts, who began this work of annihilation, and still persevered in executing it, contrary to the solemn stipulations of treaties lately entered into, just when a new constitution enthusiastically received, had presented every guarantee of security, the former want of which, having served to give an air of legitimation to the first spoliations *)

---

*) Treaty of alliance between Prussia and Poland of the 18 November 1788; new Polish constitutional act of the 3d of May 1791.

External aggrandizement according to square miles, and numerical population; and internal considerations, as far as they could afford means of attaining the object in view, — are in short, the features of these unnatural principles. This oeconomical digestion of an administration merely of things, but not of persons, could even have been termed excellent in its kind. Taken in this point of view, the Prussian government gave the most splendid proofs, of the beneficial results which may be attained by mechanism. Austria and Russia had followed this example, and it required later events to prove, that the calculation is not always correct, that a standing army, forming a state in the state, is the only support, and rallying point of a government, and that no system is safe, but that which is founded on the internal strength and unanimity of the people.

At the same time, that the commencement of the dismemberment of Poland took place, the daring Gustavus the Third, in the North, had signalized the entrance of his reign, by a revolution *), which was intended to restore that power and consequence to the royal authority, which was sunk down to a mere shadow of form, and to guard his kingdom torn by factions, against similar evils. If he had succeeded in attaching the

---

*) Carried into effect the 19 August 1772.

interets, and affections of all classes of his subjects
to his person, as he had to his new constitution,
and had he been able to preserve himself unpolluted
from the pestilence of a thirst after aggrandizement
abroad, his government, in many respects most ad-
mirable, would have had greater consequences for
his people, and his life have remained in perfect
security. —

The D a n i s h-S t a t e, preserved from the above
evil, partly by the mild government of its rulers,
harmonizing with the kind character of the nation,
presented the most stiking proof, that it is possible,
for the most liberal principles of administation, to
exist by the side of an absolute form of government,
if they are supported by the confidence and love of
the people. Notwithstanding, the fall of Struensee
in 1772, shewed, that even under this form of government, subordinate arbitrary measures, are not
tolerated, which are at variance with the customs
and feelings of the nation. The commencement of
a number of internal conquests, won from the soil
and the industry of its inhabitants, characterized
the latter period of the eighteenth century, in which
this state gained that strength and those resources,
which kept it from sinking, on its being forcibly
hurried along in the vortex of the events of the
world, at the beginning of the present century. —

To the South East, was situated the empire
of the Osmans, — a continual heterogeneous ingre-
dient in the European national confederacy — and
engaged in one constant conflict with Russia, who
had lately deprived her of the Crim, and perhaps
had in view the restitution of the Byzantinian empire. — Still, the later wars af the Porte with her
and Austria, shewed, that the fall of the Turkish
state, was by no means so near at hand, as was at
that time supposed; it would, however, hardly
be able to withstand, the united attack of Christian
Europe, at peace within herself —

The states and tribes in Asia and Africa,
to which Turkey, possessing similar laws and
forms of government, makes the transition, remain,
agreable to the point of view we have chosen, as
chaotic masses in the back ground of the picture we
are sketching. They are not yet arrived at that state,
in which a proper impulse from the enlightened
field of intelligence, could be given them, and are
only to be regarded as physical powers in relation
to the civilized world. Their extensive territories,
as far as European power and cunning have been
able to subject them, have been broken up and explored, as lands and mines, for the benefit of the
Lords of the world, as has also been the case with
the islands in the Indian seas, and the continent of
British - East India. Those states, which have

Sugar plantation on the Island of St. Croix in the West Indies

Port and city of Philadelphia

Langelinie. Port of Copenhagen, 1794

Napoleon's retreat from Moscow, 1812

preserved their freedom against foreign attempts, are, (as China and Japan) with the exception of a few commercial establishments on their most distant boundaries, completely isolated, or, as Arabia, Persia, and the Barbary states, present a picture of constant internal dissentions, and of defensive wars, or of predatory invasions directed against their neighbours. There are yet in this part of the globe, immense tracts, which have remained wholly impenetrable to the spirit of European discovery, of which we have very uncertain knowledge; founded solely on the questionable authority of persons merely engaged in an extensive caravan trade. But the time is perhaps not distant, when these regions will also be explored, to be subservient only, in the first place, to the avarice of the cultivated world, but to become gradually partakers of the benefits, of a truly humane existence. Much will depend in this respect, upon the final results of those events of the world, the origin of which, we have sketched out, and the developement of which, it is our object now, to view in a nearer light. —

III.

In the above picture, we have endeavoured to portray the situation of the world in a political point of view, at the time, the breaking out of the North-American disturbances gave the minds of men, a new direction. America became independant, on account of her being animated, by a spirit, whose powerful energies, — as a novel appearance in real life — Europe knew not how to appreciate; for England looking upon a successful issue of the attempts at emancipation, as impossible, treated her full-grown foster-children contemptuously, as if they never could become of age; France, carelessly viewing futurity, and gratifying, more her rivality against Britain, than listening to the common interest of all mother-countries, sent the rebellious colonies assistance, and Spain, unsuspicious enough, not to foresee, that the flames must once reach her own possessions on the new continent, followed the example of France. The unanimous efforts of all naval powers, who had colonial interests at stake, would have rendered the complete emancipation of the Insurgents, difficult, if not impossible *). This

---

*) It is not unknown to the author, that highly respectable politicians, have considered the loss of the colonies, as a gain for Englands mercantile

being obtained, the ‚impulse that had been given, shewed its effects in a quite different manner in the New State, than the developement of the same spirit did, which occurred later in Europe. In the whole extensive territories of the colonies, there existed no prerogative rights, but which had been granted under the English dominion, and which must cease with it. For the rest, there was a complete open field; neither the immunities of an ancient hereditary nobility, nor the privileges of a reigning church, nor the difference of colour as in South America, presenting obstacles to a new organization; for at that time the whites constituted alone the citizens of the state. But where no hindrance, prevents the developement of a given tendency, it proceeds, impelled by its innate powers, to the borders of possibility; therefore the freedom of the individual was extended as far, as the conditions of a community living together under one form of government would admit of; and the sovereign

---

grandeur, and that experience hitherto, has undoubtedly justified this assertion. But in how far this principle will hold good, in the long-run, and in its general application to the whole colonial system, will be more clearly shewn, by the results of the present investigation.

(5)

privileges of the separate states as far, as was consistent
with the interests of their union in one state body.

In order to be able to effect all this and in
short, undisturbed, to model the new internal forms
of government, it was a circumstance decidedly favorable, that an inconsiderable population of
something about three millions was spread over a
surface of 46872 geographical square miles, being
but 64 souls to one mile; nor did the greater
towns and more populous districts even, com-
prehend such a mass of numbers, as to produce
any serious collision, or violent ebullition *).
In the towns, the people were also too much occupied with trade, in the country with forming new
settlements, and bringing them under cultivation,
and too much isolated in their communication, to
give birth to such a political party spirit, as could
be injurious to the progress of the commonwealth.
Thus it happend, that the P e o p l e, as the fountain
of all power, were placed at the head of all the

---

*) Humboldt states the superficial contents of the
North American United States, without Louisiana,
and the western Indian territories wholly uncul-
tivated, at the breaking out of the revolntion,
at 73120 French square miles of 25 to the degree, which make 46872 geographical square
mile of 15 to the degree. Essai politique &c.
II. p. 87.

different institutions; which privilege, seemed to
emanate from the rights of man. But the plain
understanding of the majority, only viewing in this,
the decisions of sound common sense, and not points
of controversy, which could serve unruly factions for
a standard, had little or no conception of the
weighty theories, or of the political errors arising
from them, which this measure produced. In other
respects, the former model of the British constitution
was taken as a pattern, in the formation of that of
the United States, only transfoming the sovereign
power of the crown, into the functions of a President answerable for his conduct. —

The sequel has shewn, that the form of government fashioned after the above manner, was well
suited to the real interests of the people, and the
local nature of their territory; and history is unable to produce a more evident proof, than what
North America presents, of the truth, that in order
to develope the energies of a nation quickly and
from all sides, the removing of every obstacle, and
the full enjoyment of independance, and property,
are alone requisite. Instead of the original 13
united states, the Union, in the forty third year
of its independance, now consits of 21; instead of
47,000 square miles, its territory including Louisiana, and the Western states and districts continually encreasing in cultivation, contains 156200

square miles; the population has risen from near 5 to 10 millions.

The new spirit of emancipation, and the theory of the rights of man, must shew their effects quite differently in Europe, on their results being once applied to common life and the organism of the states. Here was not the question of throwing off a dominion exercised beyond the sea , which being neither known, nor loved by the people, could only have influence on them, by means of its representatives, — and of substituting for such, a central power in the heart of the country; here the question must rather be, of a complete revolution of the standing order of things, which appeared in the light of, or were felt as so many abuses. — The more the people, excluded from all practical participation in the executive government, inclined to the side of theory, to put which into practice, no positive legitimate means presented themselves; the more dangerous, must the example of a new state-constitution be, founded on flattering doctrines which held out a so much wished for independance. More particularly, when it was imprinted on discontented minds, feeling themselves oppressed on every side, and viewing no hope of relief in the real and standing order of things, but still more, when there were enlightened men amongst them who had not alone viewed the developement of the

new doctrines on the trans-atlantic continent, but
who had fought for their establishment, and had
brought back a lively and lasting impression of such
to their own countries. Unfortunately for Europe,
this was the case in F r a n c e, where, according to
the picture, we have drawn of this kingdom, every
thing was inclined and ripe for innovations, the
sparks of which, the government itself had kindled
by the assistance afforded the British colonies, which
could not but set fire to the highly impregnated
combustible matter. For the government, instead
of concentrating around it, all the physical and
moral powers it had at command, and instead of, at
the critical moment, going to meet the rolling storm
in a determined pace, as far as prudence might dic-
tate, staggered at one time, between the maxims of
a haughty repulsive autocracy, at another between
those of an unseasonable submission, and could
not devise the means even, in its innermost councils, of throwing a veil over the dilapidated state of
the finances, which first compromised the dignity
of the crown. However favorable this weakness was
for the innovators, and however favorable the voice
of the seditious multitude was to their plans, of
substituting in lieu of the existing system, more
popular forms, which at that time were less perfectly combined, than darkly sketched out; yet even,
at the first meeting of the Notables, who were

called together in the early part of 1787, to delibe‑
rate how the deficit in the public income might be
covered, it was evident, with what greater difficul‑
ties, and of a quite different nature, than what
America had to contend with, an undertaking of this
sort would be attended with, in an ancient state.
In wishing to create political rights as a
counterpoise, to remedy and prevent administra‑
tive abuses for the future, the innovators ne‑
cessarily came in collision with the useful pri‑
vileges and honorable prerogatives of the
nobility, the clergy, and of the venerable civil cor‑
porations. Even the shadows of the provincial con‑
stitutions, which in peaceable times were of no con‑
sequence, were again called into action, and by
endeavoring on the one side, to undermine the so‑
vereignty, and even the existence of the throne; on
the other, the zeal for the church, and the heredi‑
tary romantic attachment to the ancient Royal
house and the rights of the crown, were fanned
into an open flame in the breasts of those, who
viewed not the failings and infirmities of these ob‑
jects, through the sacred veil of inviolability, which
surrounded them. The mischief of the factions was
encreased by an evil, wholly unknown in America;
by a multitude of idle consumers in an immense
capital, which also contained a starving populace,
ready for a trifling recompence, to commit every

excess, to which a dazzling name was prefixed; further by the impetuosity of the national character,
particularly towards the South, which, however
easily it might have been curbed by proper energetic measures, as soon as the reins were slackened,
finding no counterpoise to every unbridled passion,
burst out into more boisterous violence, and instead
of freeing itself from the yoke of superfluous
pressure, endeavored to break through, and throw
off, all the necessary burthens of a people constitu-
ting a state. If we add to these ground-lines, the
intrigues of a depraved court, who viewed the change
of system, with the same indifference, as they did
that of a minister, and, the personal character of
the monarch, who, possessed of great goodness of
heart, yet, wanting the necessary firmness, at critical moments, allowed the levellers sufficient time,
systematically to corrupt the minds of the people,
to render even the fidelity of the army doubtful,
and by a continual oscillation in his resolutions
and measures, made it impossible for his adherents to back them by any consistent plans, and to
support the throne with effect; if we moreover add,
that the rest of Europe, alarmed for the maintenance of the ancient system, could not remain an
idle spectator of the fermentations in France, nor
suffer the maxims of the new reformers of the world
to pass unnoticed; it must be evident, that a

declaration of the rights of man, published under such circumstances, must be throwing oil into the flames; that the attempt at effecting a total reform in the state after the model of America, must carry with it, the overthrow of all legal barriers, and that if in the latter country, liberty had been able to develope itself, until its furthermost limits, in the former, destruction, once set loose, must rage without intermission, and every social tie be dissolved, ere some new principle of power, could put a stop to it. —

But this principle, the men in power called to life themselves, by raising an army, it is true, for quite different purposes, which, absorbing much fermenting matter, left them more at liberty at home; but which should force the neighboring nations abroad, with fire and sword a to become partakers of the blessings of fraternity in the kingdom of freedom and equality- —

For it was alone the free determination of the rulers of those times, or rather the apparent necessity of affording on the one hand, an honorable vent to the excited passions', and on the other, of surrounding the borders of the republic, with filial-states modelled after the new forms, in order to render it more inaccessible to the apprehended attack of the ancient powers, and not a hostile understanding of these, nor the influence of emigrants,

which kindled the dreadful war *). — The inde-
cision which at that time prevailed in the different
cabinets, would have caused them to remain calm
spectators of even worse occurrences, than had happened hitherto, in order the better, undisturbedly
to follow up their plans directed against the East,
and to guard their territories, against the entrance
of the new doctrines, by isolating the inflammable
matter, whilst France was internally desolating
herself **). Forcibly drawn in, they conducted
their cause, according to the ancient tactics, against
a nation, pouring forth masses of combatants never
before beheld, sufficiently unfortunate, as to procure the leaders in France, the most complete
triumph; misled in the first place by a contempt
of their opponents, afterwards seized by a panic
terror, at home and abroad, they never were united
within themselves, being at the same time unaccom-

---

*) Declaration of war against Austria the 20th April
1792, against Great Britain the 1st Febry. 1793.
**) Brissot had uttered in a memorable speech, in
the Jacobin club, already on the 30th Decr. 1791,
that the imbecility of the crowned heads, had
rendered it a point of necessity in them to ad-
here to a peaceable System, and that the
French nation must hasten in "challenging them."

panied by the wishes, and even attended by the secret disgust of their own subjects. —

For what the rulers in France had in view, happened agreable to their most sanguine expectations. The army partly animated for the cause itself, for which it fought, or at least only mindful in the field, of the duties of the soldier, allowed the factions, which were continually contending at home for dominion, the greatest scope of action; ever obedient to the impulse of the acknowledged authority, it surrounded France with new republics, called into life, by the parole orders of generals on the Rhine, in the Netherlands and in Italy, and enriched the mother-country with treasures, which she offered up at the shrine of liberty, grateful for her beneficent effects. —

Only by degrees, but as a necessary consequence of events, the spirit of the army became changed, and laid the foundation of a new order of things in France. During the government of the Terrorists, when internal anarchy ruled with the most ghastly sway, and every idea of constitution and rights, and security of life and property, seemed to be annihilated, — there existed alone in the army, still a sense of justice, of honor, and a legal coherence, — whilst noble feelings clung to the recollection of warlike deeds already atchieved, and fondly pictured the glorious scenes, which innate

power and worth seemed to prognosticate for the
future. — Thus his native country presenting no
longer a rallying point, the camp became the republican's country and the honor of the soldier, as
such, the object of all his efforts; every one, who
had still the choice left, preferring the service of
the army, to that of his household gods. And moreover, on the new Constitution being at length put
into force in September 1795, which appeared, purposely to have been so constructed, that it must
shortly subvert itself, by the friction of its compo-
nent parts badly fitting in each other, and render
all civil administration contemptible; whereas, at
the same time, a young, eminently daring leader,
who irresistably commanded the confidence of his
associates, and who was strewing his career, daily
with fresh laurels, shone at the head of the army;
then it was, that civism was obliged to yield to the
glorious sound of victory's shouts, and all respect
and veneration for the laws and institutions, which
by the continual change of parties, were sunk into
mere fleeting phoenomena, must be lost, in admiration and attachment to the warlike chief, who
pointed to victory in the front, and to distinction,
riches and enjoyment in the back ground. And
Napoleon Buonaparte, united in his own
person, more than all the splendid names did,
which shine so bright in the annals of French mili

tary renown, all the qualities, necessary, for accomplishing the daring work, of transforming France into a military autocracy; even Moreau, the greatest after him, would only have been a renowned citizen, in a happy republic. If he succeeded in gaining the affections of his troops and even the respect of his enemies, Napoleon understood to exite, we might almost say, a fanatical confidence in the necessary success of all his projects, and by the violent rapidity of his enterprises, and the continual change of the seat of his warlike deeds, to enchain the fiery spirit of a nation, more prone than any other, to be dazzled by good fortune. Even his foreign Corsican nature, assisted him in imposing on the multitude, and removed to a distance, that intimate familiarity, which militates against a rising ascendancy, not intended to make use of mankind for the purposes of a reciprocal communication, but as the means of attaining its ends; a national Frenchman, would hardly have succeeded in raising himself to the height Napoleon stood on. But it was not his character alone, still less any conscious struggling after some precise aim, but the course of events, which raised him on high, and assisted him to develope that, which lay obscurely hidden in his breast. Let it have been a restless thirst after fresh military atchievements, or a correct presentiment of coming events, which caused him to invade the East with a chosen army, after the tranquillity of the European continent seemed sufficiently established by the peace of Campo Formio *), Prussia and Spain **), having long since retired from the contest, and the Italian states being bound down by treaties; — he could never, under the influence of the deepest calculation, have chosen a career, which would have led him surer to the attainment of the aim, of reappearing shortly, as the man who was universally looked for, and who was become absolutely necessary. —

It became every day more evident, what must become of France, since the 18th of Fructidor, (the 5th of September 1797) which forced Carnot possessed of the most preponderating talents, and Barthelemy of peaceable sentiments and a wish for a return to conciliating measures, from the helm of government. — The opposition of the two councils was become speechless, and coarse pride, the constant attendant of mediocrity invested with power, was prominent in all the discussions of the Directory, breathing insult, and threatening danger to all Europe. At the commencement of the year 1798, Swisserland, which had hitherto escaped untouched by every

---

*) Concluded ths 17th October 1797.
**) By the treaties of Basel on the 5th April and 22d July 1795.

storm, was inundated by a predatory army, and
instead of the venerable ancient confederation, one
single indivisible Helvetic republic was proclaimed
there; not, in order to render the freeest people in
Europe more happy, but by means of this unity, to
prepare them more quickly for requisitions and
contributions of every nature. —

A popular tumult in Rome was considered sufficient, to overturn the papal-chair erected on the
subverted throne of the Cæsars, and to organize a
Roman republic; a similar event in Vienna, was
the cause, or more properly only a pretext, for the
French ambassador leaving that capital, whereby
the negociations in Rastadt were put a stop to,
which by the peace of Campo-Formio were to have
given a definitive developement to the Germanic
state-body. In Italy revolutionizing continued
without intermission to be the order of the day;
already in December 1798, the King of Sardinia was
obliged to abdicate his continental territories, and
on the 25th of January 1799 Championnet proclaimed
in Naples the Parthenopian republic.

Buonaparte, had in the mean time, in order to
throw a lustre on the French arms in a distant
quarter, left the port of Toulon, and directed his
course eastwards; with the quickness of lightning
had conquered Malta, in a way, not satisfactorily
cleared up to this day, and had landed his army in

Ægypt. Apparently unconcerned that Russia, whose new ruler seemed more determined, than any of his royal cotemporaries, to excercise a sovereign sway, and had since his coming to the throne (in 1796), been forming plans, to put an effectual barrier, to the inundations of the French power, and the new doctrines, — was up in arms, on account of the conquest of the above island; that the Porte, the oldest ally of France, had followed her example, exasperated at the invasion of her territories, and that the flower of the French navy had been sacrificed to destruction, by the British at Aboukir; — he continued following up his plans of conquest, acted the part of the sovereign *), to the greatest perfection, which had often in Italy involuntarily, as it were, burst from him, and accustomed his adherents to look upon him in this light, but upon themselves as daily more and more the instruments of His will, which was not subservient to any higher national impulse. But on the flames of war, bursting forth over all Europe in the spring of 1799, and, notwithstanding the great sacrifice which had been made at Rastadt, by the cession of

---

*) It is well known, that Napoleon suffered himself to be saluted with cannon in Italy, and with all the etiquette usual on the reception of the Roman Emperors.

the left bank of the Rhine to France, Jourdan had
passed that river, on the 1st of March the Russian
armies had entered Austria, and from the Rhine
to the Nile, yes, even to the Jordan, peace was
vanished from the face of the earth and the ocean;
— and on France, having lost in this disastrous
campaign, the whole of Italy, with the single exception of Genua, also the former Venetian islands,
and the countries situated on the coast of the Levant;
on the Roman and Parthenopian Republics being
destroyed, and the Cisalpine one, again transformed into an Austrian province; — on the internal
welfare of France being exhausted, her trade and
navigation ruined and her navy annihilated; —
the Only man returned *), with a few trusty associates, on whom the eyes of all were turned, as the
constellation of salvation. He addressed the Directory, and the legislative body in the tone of a master,
who returning from abroad, calls his servants to
account; and overthrew in the course of a month **)
with very little trouble, a constitution, which having
been frequently violated was become despicable to
the people. The representatives of the nation were
driven out and dispersed by soldiers, and the first

---

*) He landed on the 9th of October 1799 in the post
of Frejus.

**) The 18th of Brumaire, the 9th of Nov. 1799.

onsul, clothed with all the exuberance of power, as placed preliminarily for ten years, at the head a military government, but thinly disguised nder civil forms. But'ere the lapse of three years, is power was extended, for his life time *), and order that the name might not be wanting to e Imperator, and that the edifice he had erected his spirit, might stand for centuries to come, the nate after the lapse of other two years, proclaimed im Emperor on the 18th May 1804, and confirmed y vote, on the 1st Dec. of the same year, the crown s hereditary in the Dynasty of Napoleon.

The people, for so many years torn by divisions, endered tame by the horrors of anarchy, disappoint-d in all their ideas of a better order of things, of e liberty of the citizen, and a national represent-tion, which had been so infamously abused, and isgusted with foreign wars, and internal privations, ere struck with astonishment, and acquiesced in very thing, even partially hailing a change of overnment, with ardor, which promised peace, and settled order **) in the state; and uniting the hopes f the return of the good old times, with the return

---

*) Senatus consultum of the 3d of August 1802.
**) Fixity; a word much used at that time, to re-
commend monarchy, and the heredetary throne.

of external splendor, which now surrounded th
centre of his government, they hailed their ne
emperor with all the ecstacy of joy.

Thus then, were all the efforts that had bee
used in France, towards the attainment of independ
ance and true national representation, after havin,
made the most horrid digressions from the poin
they started, returned to the monarchial form o
government, and, as is not otherwise imaginabl
after such catastrophies, to a complete military des
postism, by the side of which, all forms of politica
freedom, being empty shadows, were thrown o
at pleasure, as soon as they commenced to be incon
venient *).

The tendency towards democratic institutions
had reached the rest of Europe, from France, bu
it partook, upon the whole, more of the successiv
revolution of ideas internally in the minds of men
than followed the example of the above country, i
open acts of violence; but still the sensation had no
imperceptibly passed by. Aspiring heads immediatel

---

*) All the constituted powers, were remodelled, by th
   organic Senatus Consultum of the 18th of May 1804
   the T r i b u n a t e, which had already been depri
   ved, of the power of discussing in full assembly
   any projected new laws, was abolished the 18th
   of Septbr. 1807.

mbraced with enthusiasm, the tenets of the revo-
ution, and whilst the more circumspect were coolly
waiting the results, the more fiery, had hastened
o hail in person, the approach of the new and
appy order of things. —

A dangerous spirit shewed itself not alone
n the countries bordering on the Rhine, — in Hol-
and, Italy, and even in Great Britain, particularly
n Ireland, which had cause of complaint of being
eglected, before the intimate union with the
ister-island took place, which Pitt accomplished
n the year 1800; and preparations were most zea-
ously made in these countries, for the formation of
lial republics; even in Spain and Russia, it was
onsidered necessary, by severe measures to prevent
he clandestine introduction of the seductive poison.
ut France presented, in herself, the most powerful
ntidote to the more extensive propagation of popu-
ar insurrections, having, on the road she had
rodden, arrived at a state of the most lamentable
narchy, instead of that, of peace and happiness;
nd having loaded the provinces, which had been
onquered by the force of arms for the cause of li-
erty and equality, with the evils of infinite in-
ernal dissentions, attended with the external pres-
ure of a foreign military force and intolerable
xtortions. Thus is happened, that the attachment,
hich had originally been shewn to the new

doctrines, began in the first place visibly to cool,
but, on very naturally confounding the theory with
its infamous application, called into life by the
most depraved wickedness, and every unbridled
passion, it went over to the most decided abhorrence;
under the impression of such sentiments, the return
of France, to the monarchial form of government,
served in fact to strengthen the different thrones,
and to give the desired support to the most consum-
mate despotism, which Napoleon very soon exercised. For although the new emperor in impressing
on the minds of his subjects the power which sym-
bolically belongs to the crown, and the principle, that
all are dependant on the will of the ruler, who alone
is every thing, the people being but his means, but
too willingly copied, with the most scrupulous exactitude, the example of the ancient courts, without
being able to attain their dignity; he yet sur-
passed them beyond all measure, in the application
of the principle, that in the state, there must exist
but one will, independant of which, all things are
mere instruments; and this he carried through regardless of all obstacles. No monarch has ever understood or exercised, as He did, the art of reducing
at once every thing to calculation, of playing with
men, as with figures; of appropriating to himself
not alone the results of the various sciences, but all
the productions of the natural and corporeal powers,

as if they were alone intended for his purposes, and of keeping the whole harmoniously in play, by a mechanism, the springs of which a single thought set at work. And if the ancient cabinets strove more and more to round and centralize their different territories, and forcibly to draw their nearest environs into the sphere of their attraction, — he embraced them jointly in his system of calculation, and had in view, the project of raising himself to the central point of the whole European world. The situation, in which he found France, rendered it undoubtedly necessary for him to tighten and hold with iron hand the reins of a government, which could only recommend itself, but by the restoration of public order and the regular course of things. This necessity, cooperating with the voice of an immense majority, who approved of every thing, (however unjustifiable) which promised internal peace, and glory and riches at the expence of countries abroad; assisted him, in the commencement, in disguising his passion for the most arbitrary despotism and the exercice of it, and in rendering himself popular with the multitude. —

Those governments, which still commanded respect, excused many a daring step, which French politics, strove to represent with all the art of diplomatic sophistry, as measures only extorted from them, to humble the proud continental enemy, but not as means of self-aggrandizement, — on account of the indignatlon, generally felt in the minds of men, at the efforts Great, Britain had been long making, to obtain the unlimited dominion of the seas, and the envy, not so just, but still universal, at the constant encreasing prosperity of her trade, and manufacturing industry. —

On this ladder, the Emperor rose step by step, to absolute ruler of his kingdom, extended by him on every side, and to actual Dictator of the rest of Europe; who either immediately obeyed his protectoral commands, or were obliged to pursue the system he had directed against England, from the furthermost borders of the Baltic to the shores of the Mediterranean, — being the emblem of his superior power, and authority. He maintained himself in this position, as long as the mechanism of his state organization, (more powerfully ordered, that that of any other country) had to contend with material obstacles, which the governments opposed to it in standing armies; and foundered at length on the awakened Spirit of the nations. This he had never calculated upon, but which he had summoned up against him, more by the public insolent scorn, he had railed at, denying at it were, the existence of all the feelings of independance, and of the deeply-rooted affection, every nation feels in its heart, for its country and what is venerable

to it, — than, by the intolerable misery, the countries groaned under, by the pressure of his military
despotic government. His fall, and what has been
effected by it, are attended with too many consequences, not to be deserving of a separate chapter.

IV.

Napoleon fell, not when kings and armies
alone, but when nations were opposed to him, who
were animated by a leading principle, grown into
an irrevocable determination, of rather enduring
the worst, than his dominion; he fell when the
ignominious subjugation of some, and that which
notoriously threathened others, obliged the Monarchs, to look to their people — no longer alone
to their military, so often conquered and so great-
ly humbled — for salvation, and to collect their
subjects en masse, animated with the greatest confidence, around their native princes, as the proper
rallying point. In his own people, long since transported by emphatic phrases from one state of exalt-
ation to another, grown weary of flowery harangues,
and in the excess of exhaustion, incapable of a far-

ther enthusiastic elasticity, he had nothing similar to oppose, to such an universal inspiration, as the above, which exceeded all the limits of calculation.

In Spain, whose just national pride, he had deeply wounded, and by which he had again roused, to the most romantic height, the otherwise luke-warm attachment to the reigning Dynasty, in the persons of which, the nation saw itself robbed of the symbols of its independance, — he, who was hi-therto considered invincible, lost the renown of his invulnerability; here he was obliged to relinquish his first plan, and occasioned hundred thousands of his adherents an inglorious death. The wish of drawing off the eyes of the world from what had happened, and was happening daily there, was undoubtedly a principal reason, for his projected designs against Russia, being brought sooner to ma-turity than otherwise. By the most gigantic exer-tions of the resources of his empire, he meant, by one blow, to render the resistance, he had ever dreaded from the East and the North, impossible for the future; in order (when Russia was driven back upon Asia, and the Allies, who were now fight-ing his battles, were become virtually, if not no-minally his vassals) to accomplish his aim in the West, with less difficulty.

No one will deny, on comparing the warlike resources, which stood at his command, with those of his opponent, viewed in the ordinary light, but that the calculation was bold, and by no means ill-founded ; neither will it appear strange, that even Napoleon, supporting the character, he had once assumed, must think it necessary for him, in the situation he then was, to put every thing at stake. His premises were alone faulty in two things: his army was no longer the republican one, such as had fought in Italy under him, and in Germany under Moreau; more shew than substance, it exhibited externally much of the ostentation and the splendor of an oriental host, and its interior, was no longer grounded on national and martial honor, but on rapine, plunder and despotic insolence; — as to the character of the people, he was about to attack on their own soil, he was more shamefully mistaken, and still more unfortunately so, with regard to the local and physical nature of the country.

Instead of barbarous hordes who would hasten at the first hint, to throw off an oppressive yoke, he met with a people, not inferior to the Spaniard in religious unanimity, in attachment to their native soil, and in making an unconcerned sacrifice of all earthly goods for its defence; and what they might be deficient in pride of independance, and a romantic recollection of former atchievments, was more than overbalanced, by their most devout

(8)

attachment to their Ruler, looked upon as their common father, and in whom they had placed a boundless confidence; he also met with a government, which had solemnly declared, it would stand or fall with its people; which, unshaken by the smoking ruins of Moscow, and even by the danger which seemed to threaten Petersburg, withstood all the allurements held out for peace, relying wholly on God and its people *). The unprecedented conflagration of the capital, which rendered a longer residence in it impossible, was the signal of destruction for the proud conqueror, and the power of the elements, in alliance with the just cause, assisted in annihilating under the most inexpressible miseries, quicker than human hands would have been able to effect, an army, which had not had its equal in the annals of European warfare. But even independant of the winter, it is unlikely that the new Sesostris would have escaped the destruction, which, the unanimity and the enormous resources of the Russian empire, now first collected, and pouring forth one army after the other, had prepared for him in front, and which the revolt of the different nations, whom under the most repugnant feelings, he

---

*) See the emperor Alexander's Manifestos, of the 18th of July and of September 1812 after the burning of Moscow. —

had forcibly allied to his banners, was ready to over-
whelm him with, in the ｜R e a r. —

Already long-ago every thing had been prepared secretly in Prussia, to be able to rise in arms,
when the day of vengeance should appear; being
the country of all those crushed by the superior
power of Napoleon, the one, which united the greatest intelligence, with the deepest sense, of the unpar-
donable insults, and the flagrant disgrace, which had
sullied its military honor. — In doing this, the
people acted unsummoned, well knowing for what
purpose, although the government could not yet
publicly proclaim it, being obliged slowly to follow
the course of events, — but at the same time, throwing no obstacles in the way of these patriotic efforts,
which were always capable of having a double construction placed upon them, as long as a direct tendency, was not given to them, by the high authorities of the state. Even York's celebrated convention,
concluded on the 30th December 1812 in the Pos-
cherung mill, which for the first time unequivocally
shewed, (and too-hastily according to diplomatic
principles), that the sentiments of the army were in
unison with those of the people, — could not hasten,
the wise delay of the government; although every
heart which beat for its country knew, to which
side the mind of the king inclined, and all acted
agreable to this conviction. But on the Russians,

who had pursued the enemy, without intermission,
since October, having pressed forward to the Oder,
having driven the remnant of the French army behind the Elbe, and having liberated the country
from Memel to Berlin, then it was, that the king's
public appeal to his people and his army, on the
11th March, appeared, and united, in an indisso-
luble league, for the deliverance of Europe, the
rulers of Russia and Prussia, who entered Breslau
or the 15th of the same month, some of the kindred
German princes, immediately joining the alliance. —

Austria went slower to work. She remained
for a considerable time, in a respectable posture, a
spectator of the course of events, arming herself in
the mean time, in order, (let the issue be what it
would) to be able to hold the balance of power.
She would willingly have mediated a peace, which
would have deprived France of her prepondance in
Germany, and confined her within proper limits,
but which also would have rendered Russia's advancing towards the West, (which was certainly beheld
with distrust at first,) unnecessary, and which would
have kept back the rising power of Prussia, on the
point of it's complete developement. She required
also time to reestablish her military resources, exhausted by former exertions, upon such a footing,
as to give her a weight, suitable to her dignity.
But on Russia and Prussia, having during the half

of 1813, sufficiently shewn their zeal in following
up the just cause, having evinced the power and
hardiness of their armies, and the talents of their
generals; on England *), having by treaty, ensured
their exertions, the necessary aliment, and powerful
assistance from Spain and Portugal; and lastly, on
it being sufficiently evident, by the course of the
proceedings at the Congress at Prague, that Napoleon, whose arts were now completely seen through,
only intended to gain time, but not to recede the
least from his plans, and who, still only keeping in
view the mere calculation of numbers, thought, by
an imposing numerical superiority of combatants,
to keep the South and West of Germany attached to
his cause; — the upright emperor then declared
war on the 11th August against the haughty usurp-
er of the Supremacy in Germany, disregarding
with a noble self-denial, all the ties, even the intimate
one of consanguinity, which seemed to bind him to
the interets of France, and formed a sphere of attraction, which, before the end of the year united all
the states of the Rhinish Confederation, — Bavaria
first, the lesser ones after the decisive battle ef Leipsic — with the universal cause of freedom and of
Germany. —

_____

*) Treaty of Reichenbach the 15th June 1813.

The armies of the allies, now rapidly crossed the Rhine the last days of the departing year, and in the first ones of 1814, in order to bring-the war against Napoleon, in France itself, to a decisive conclusion. His dethronement, and the restoration of the ancient dynasty, could on no account already at that time, have been the object they had in view. The emperor stood yet too powerful amidst fresh armies he had levied, to warrant such an intention; and on the Northern and Eastern frontiers, and in the interior of the country, the sense of the people was by no means such, as to promise cooperation, or even approbation of these measures. On the contrary, all who were capable of bearing arms, and could reach the seat of war time enough, hastened to the defence of the paternal soil, and Napoleon conducted these resources, with such surprising talents of generalship, as to throw the allies, more than for the moment, into a state of visible embarrassment, and at least, to convince them most clearly, of the possibility of the failure of their operations. But proud intoxication at partial successes, which ever characterized Napoleon, filled him, with a confidence in the present case, which led him to his destruction. —

In the midst of the tumults of war, a congress had been opened at Chatillon, since the 6th February 1814, which pointed out a peace to France, that would have left her more powerful, than she had been before the revolution. But on the appearance of a return of good fortune, and imagining nothing less than the annihilation of the enemy, he reject-ed with impetuosity, all the proposals, that were made him, and which according to circumstances, were very moderate. A general insurrection of the peasantry, which he intended to support by ma-noevering in the rear of the allies, and the loyalty and obstinate defence of the capital, — were the ground-pillars of his hopes. With regard to the latter, at least, he had been mistaken; it is more than probable, that without a powerful faction in Paris, ready for capitulation, and inimical to the continuation of Napoleon's dominion, the allies would not have ventured upon their hazardous march, nor have seen it crowned which success. The city did not perform, what the emperor expected, nor what his Lieutenant, Joseph had promised; and three months after the passage of the Rhine (the 31st March) the allies entered it. The Bourbons follow-ed, close upon their steps; on the 6th of April Napoleon abdicated the French throne, and on the 3d of May, Louis the eighteenth appeared in Paris, without acknowledging the Constitution of the 6th April, by power of which, the conservative Senate, would have had him proclaimed King. On the other hand, by a solemn treaty *), the late emperor, was not only to retain his title and dignity, but to enjoy the full sovereignty of the island of Elba, which he had chosen for his future residence. The circumstance even of his being again formally received into the list of monarchs, shewed, that the allies were unable to act entirely with consistency, and instead of fighting the matter out, followed a system of composition, which in the sequel, rendered it impossible for the new government to bring to an advantageous issue. It might also at that time easily have been foreseen, that Napoleon, who assuredly possessed sufficient resources to continue the conflict, only had considered it more prudent to withdraw himself for the moment, in order to come forward again, under better auspices, on France, after the allies had retired, being left to herself. Under these circumstances France obtained a peace **), such as she never could have expected, had it not been for the considerations, which were grounded on the facility, with which the allies, by means of a secret understanding, had entered Paris, and the conquerors left the kingdom, where the fire that had only been quenched, glowed powerfully under the ashes.

---

*) Of the 12th April 1814.
**) Peace of Paris of the 30th March 1814.

Whilst the government there, amidst the un-
ceasing conflict of all parties, — none of whom
were satisfied with the constitution promulgated by
Louis on the 4th July, was employed, in reestablishing the vehicle of state, according to the forms
of the ancient monarchy, and in uniting with it,
in the best possible manner, those institutions out
of the intermediate period, which were considered
as indispensibly necessary; those ideas began to
unfold themselves beyond the French frontiers, which
were to regulate the distribution of the spoils of the
subverted imperial state, amongst the victors, and
to determine the reorganization of Europe.

Spain, now completely liberated from the detes-
ted French yoke, partly by her own efforts, and
partly by the assistance of Great Britain and Wellington's great generalship, witnessed already on the
28th of March, the return of her sovereign to his
paternal soil, who hastened with the most penetrating firmness, to reestablish the ancient constitution.
Assured of the support of the clergy, of that, of a
part of the high nobility, and through the influence
of both these, of the approbation of the lower classes
of people, he rejected by a proclamation, given at
Valencia, on the 4th May, whither he had proceeded
until the field should be clear, the Constitution,
projected by the L i b e r a l e s, and formally published

on the 19th May 1812 by the Cortes, as the law of
the land; which entrusted the real author ty of the
government to a national assembly, leaving the Monarch, nothing but the sacred character attached
to Royalty, and the administration of the executive
power. — That this took place without more opposition, and that Ferdinand, after having arrested
on the 10th of May, the principal members of the
Cortes, and the former ministry, could make his
entry, peaceable on the 14th into Madrid, and under
public demonstrations of joy, is surely the best
proof, that the above constitution, formed after new
abstractions, was unsuitable to the reigning sentiments of the nation, and the state of cultivation, to
which it had, at that time, arrived. From this in-
stant, all things one immediately after the other,
were reorganized agreable to the ancient forms of
unlimited sovereignty; and the spiritual subjection
to the Papal chair, and the ecclesiastical and monas-
tical power, were reestablished. The time to come
will shew, whether this system of absolute restoration,
such as was carried into effect, to its greatest extent,
might not have led farther, than was first intended,
and whether, it will not be found more prudent for
the future, to adopt milder measures *).

---

*) The revolution of the 7th Marah 1820 has actu-
ally proved the inefficacy of the system hitherto

In the rest of Europe, the principle of the unconditional reestablishment of every thing old, was at least not followed up with equal rigidness, in the political forms,. given to the countries and territories, which were without masters. —

A congress of the Sovereigns was appointed to meet in the autumn of 1814, in order to regulate every thing, and to establish the new form of Europe upon a solid basis; but already in the course of the summer, some remarkable occurrences took place; Genua being incorporated with the states of Sardinia, in direct opposition to the promises made by England through Lord Bentick's proclamation *), and Flanders, being united with

─────────────

pursued. Is the Constitution that has now been adopted, likely to stand the test of time, without material alterations? — Experience teaches ns, that simplicity in the forms of executive government, is not capable of being carried into effect in large countries; even the two North - American states, in which it still existed, Pensylvania and Georgia, have renounced its retention, and have adopted the system of the two Houses; the former by its new constitution of the 2d Septbr. 1790, the latter, by its revised form of government of May 1795. —

*) Of the 26th April 1814.

H o l l a n d , now transformed into the kingdom of
the United Netherlands; which certainly took place
contrary to the cordial wishes of its inhabitants *).
There appeared, at the Congress itself, which met
towards the end of October, such contradictory
views, and such irreconcileable claims, as several
times to warrant the apprehension, that it would be
quite impossible, for any peaceable arrangement to
be brought about, the indetermination which had
hitherto shewn itself, being unable to lead to a
permanent order of things, and that it would be
necessary to have recourse to the sword, to solve the
points in dispute. The negociations regarding the
future form of Germany, the fate of Poland, Prussia's indemnification, around which the political existence of Saxony revolved, and those touching Swisserland, and the affairs of Italy, were protracted
until the end of Febry. 1815, without bringing to
light, one single clear, positive result. —

At this crisis, on the 1st of March, Napoleon
once more, — amidst the conflict of passions contending for the division of his E m p i r e **), — put

---

*) Proclamation of the new Ruler of the 1st Au-
gust 1814.

**) The difference is well known between L' E m-
p i r e F r a n ç a i s and l a F r a n c e.

his foot upon French ground. Expected by his
adherents; received with open arms by the army;
and hindered by no one; he peaceably passed through
the Eastern provinces, as far as Lions, as if he were
returned after a predetermined absence, and from
thence to Paris, which had been visited by frequent
disturbances, and a number of mimic commotions,
partly useless in themselves and partly raised design-
edly. On the evening of the 20th of March, attended only by a few, he arrived at the Thuilleries;
the night before, the king had left Paris; but an
inconsiderable number of faithful adherents had
accompanied him. —

On the news of this event, completely unex-
pected at the time it happened, having reached
Vienna, the Congress immediately found the rallying point, which it had hitherto wanted. It was
the interest of all the first-rate powers, who wished
to remain arbiters of the fate of Europe, entirely
to annihilate Him, who had now reappeared on the
stage, and on the 13th of March, in a public declaration, they brought to Protocol, their determination, of following up this interest, with all the means
which stood at their command; excluding Napoleon,
at the same time, from all the civil and social relations of society, and designating him, as the enemy
and the disturber of the peace of the world. This
anathema, which united all, should it become ne-

necessary, in a conflict of life and death against
France, once more attached by the course of events
to the cause of Napoleon, produced unanimity, and
life in the discussions of the Congress. It strove
visibly now, only to come to a preliminary agreement of the most weighty points in dispute, in
order to remove all the elements of discord, from
the allies; and reserved the final determination of
individual questions, for a future and more peaceable time. Thus was Poland divided into two parts,
between Russia and Prussia; that belonging to the
former, received the title of a kingdom of Poland,
subject, but not incorporated with the Russian monarchy; whilst the Prussian part assumed the name
of the Great Dutchy of Posen. Saxony which had
been so long the bone of contention between the
different powers, was dismembered into a kingdom,
which remained subject to the ancient ruling
family, and into a Dutchy which fell to the share
of Prussia, who obstained besides, the acquisition of
a fertile Grand - Dutchy on the left side of the Rhine.
The Dutchy of Luxemburg, was attached as a confederate state to Germany, but under the sovereignty
of the king of the Netherlands; who was thereby formally constituted a prince of the German confederation; amongst the members of the former German empire, with the exception of those princes
mediatised by the act of the confederation of the

Rhine, a German - confederation was formed, under
the supremacy of the former emperor, the constitution of which, was rather hewn out in rough masses,
than really organized for political action. Three
new cantons, the Pays Vauds, Geneva, and Neucha-
tel were added to the Swiss union; in Italy, the
union of Genua with the Sardinian state, was
finally pronounced; the Lombard and Venetian
kingdoms were again restored to the Austrian domi-
nions, Tuscany to the former Grand Duke; and Ferdinand the fourth was confirmed, by all the allied
powers, king of Naples, where Murat, had now
finished, his once brilliant career. —

These fundamental features of the future order
of things, were completed by the delegated arbiters of Europe, amidst the tumult of preparations
for war, carried on with the most unanimous zeal,
and umcommon rapidity; whilst the allied armies
under the immediate command of their sovereigns
were advancing to the French frontiers. The German act of confederation was signed on the eighth
the definitive act of the congress of Vienna, on the
9th and on the 13th of June, Napoleon crossed the
Belgic frontiers, having with the most restless activity, rendered his government popular by a reform
of the constitution, sanctioned at the splendid

64

assembly on the *) May field, and having posted an army of 150,000 combatants along the Netherlands. —

As he was ever wont to do, so did the Emperor this time act upon the offensive, and in fact had surprized his opponents. Fortune, seemed for the first days to smile upon him, but only transitorily. The glorious victory gained by the allies on the 18th June, at belle Alliance, ruined his hopes, and hurled him from the pinnacle of his greatness, more rapidly, than he had succeeded lately in remounting it. The emperor left the army, at the head of which, by acting on the defensive, he would perhaps have been able to maintain himself a long time, and to obtain a better fate; and from that moment, every endeavor to remain at the helm, as Dictator, Regent, or as a simple general, proved fruitless. The Allies advanced under Wellington and Blücher; Paris capitulated on the 5th, and was taken possession of, on the 7th July; on the following day, Louis the eighteenth, reentered the capital, once more under the Ægis of foreign bajonets. Napoleon, on every outlet of escaping to America, as he had wished, being shut up, betook himself from Rochefort the 15th of July, exactly a month after he had taken the field under

*) 1st Juni 1815.

quite different expectations, on board of the English line of battle ship the Bellerephon, which carried him to the English coasts, from whence, by a decision of the British cabinet, sanctioned by the principal powers, he was conducted to St. Helena. The peace which was concluded between the allies and the monarch once more seated on his throne, (signed at Paris on the 20th November) did not differ materially from the former one, which had obliged France, to withdraw within her ancient limits, but imposed upon her, a war contribution of 700 Million besides the burthen of an army, 150,000 men strong, which should occupy the frontier provinces, according to circumstances five, or at least thres years. —

V.

Thus then, after twenty three years of bloody revo lutions, a Louis was again seated on the throne of his forefathers, and the principles of Monarchy were firmly established in Europe. — But the principle of government, was no longer the old one, and the

(10)

spirit of the relation, in which the ruled stood to their rulers, although, it had not yet every where been brought to light in visible forms, and specified limits, was materially changed. — A common sense of necessity, had brought them nearer together, and reciprocal esteem and acknowledgement of rendered services, laid the ground of a relation between them, mutually more honorable. —

For centuries past, the m o n a r c h s had not been interwoven p e r s o n a l l y in the fate of their people, to that degree, and had not shared thus, the privations and humiliations, the domestic and public calamities of their nations, nor had thus fought by their sides, and conquered by their efforts, as they had done in the late fatal period of the world. From the uttermost Western point of Europe, to the borders of Asia, what a change of fortuue! — The ruler of Portugal transplants his royal throne, to the coasts of South America, to avoid becoming the captive of the Corsican Emperor *). The Monarch

---

*) According to the latest accounts, the seat of government and the residence of the court are to remain constantly in Brazil, and thus we have the first instance of an European kingdom, being dependant upon an American main state; but it

King Juan VI of Portugal and Brazil and his entourage in the vicinity of Rio de Janeiro, c. 1820

The Disasters of War

of Spain and of both the Indies, is obliged to pass seven years of exile, as a prisoner in France, whilst the pretender to the crown of the latter country, after tedious wanderings, first finds a safe asylum under the British sceptre. The Italian branch of the Bourbons, despoiled of half its kingdom, preserves scarcely the shadow of power in Sicily, rather governed than protected by British influence. The Father of the Faithful dies in exile, and his successor, after having made the great sacrifice, of condescending to consecrate the imperial crown of Buonaparte, is incapable of perserving his wordly territories. The German emperor, twice driven, from his conquered capital, sees his Netherlands, his Italian and Illyrian provinces fall into the hands of the victor; the venerable Roman diadem, snatched from his temples, and is obliged to marry his own daughter to the upstart monarch. The inheritance of the Great Frederic, falls to pieces, after One lost battle; and the splendor of the Prussian warlike renown, expires in the field, but more shamefully in the fortresses; individual names, and detached bodies alone preserve the sacred fire, which under greater scenes of calamity, was again to burst into flames;

---

may be allowed to question the duration of the relative situation of the two countries.

for even the assistance of the Russian hosts was inef-
fectual in a conflict, the decision of which was reserved for the people themselves. Frederic William,
driven back as far as Memel, was obliged to agree
to the cession of half his kingdom, and to the pro-
tectorship and occupation of the remainder by fo-
reigners. — The emperor of Russia, having twice
entered the lists, as adjutor and mediator of European affairs, aud twice driven bitterly from the
scene of action, by the defeats at Austerlitz and
Friedland, saw war and desolation, carried into his
own kingdom, considered from afar, incapable of
approach. In his ancient capital, the Gaul seated
himself on the throne of the Czars, and threatened
the new residence on the Neva with a speedy invasion. We make no mention of the sufferings and
emigrations of the smaller German and Italian princes; every thing was fallen to ruin, and the edifice
of ancient Europe, was rent from its foundation.
Then it was, that the insurrection of the nations en masse recovered all; and the union of princes and people melted into one heart, and one
power, making a renunciation of all benefits for the
present, and living only for the welfare of future
generations, in a thirst after independance and the
maintenance of this greatest national blessing, completed the work of liberation, from a state of the
most humiliating slavery. —

But what sacrifices did this not cost the People! Since the popular migrations of the ancient tribes, there has never been seen such distress and misery, as have reigned in the later times, from the day, on which the head of the innocent Louis fell, until the last peace of Paris. —

Amongst the several nations, who appeared upon the stage, one after the other, as the circle of destruction extended from the West, and returning back upon itself, overwhelmed France; the public welfare was ruined, the opulence of palaces plundered and destroyed, and the humble peaceable happiness ef the lowly cottage trodden under foot. Unprincipled bands of savages, seized on the property of the citizen and the peasant; bloodsuckers and upstarts of the moment, revelled on the lawless spoils. The flower of the men was slanghtered, and their choicest youths, which the different states, were obliged to put at the disposition of the sword, (as any other contribution) were annually mowed down, as the produce of the field, falls under the scythe. No house was to be found, which had escaped the universal misery, no mind free from hatred and the most bitter rancour, no heart which was not filled with lamentations and grief for the dead, as well as the living. For a fatal wound had also been inflicted upon morality; the generation sunk into wildness and barbarity; matrons and maidens were violated, male and female children grew up without a sense of decency or education, with licen-tiousness and desolation, constantly before their eyes, and the grey head sunk into the grave, surrounded by ignominy, poverty and distress.

To have banished such misery, and to have paved the way for future generations enjoying a dig-nified existence, is the united glory of the princes and their people; and having in common fought for, and won the present state of things, they ought also for the time to come, to watch with one common care, over the reestablishment and conservation of what has been gained, in order to prevent the re-turn of the ancient remissness, which was the pri-mary cause of the later misfortunes. The tendency of the present spirit of the times, aims at calling this agreement, either tacitly confirmed, or publicly acknowledged, into actual life, and which may be regarded as the foundation of the new aspect of the world. France has gained her constitutional Char-ter, by the storms of the revolution, and she will continue to enjoy a civil and political free-dom, founded on a secure basis, should even the fickleness of the nation, once more become dissa-tisfied with its present forms of government. A popular representation is stipulated as a general

law, by an act of the Diet, for each country composing the German confederation *). —

The government of the new kingdom of the Netherlands, was modelled, under the especial protection of England, according to the ancient form of
the Dutch constitution, avoiding its deformities,
which only threw obstacles in the way of an equality
of representation, and lamed the measures of the
executive power. Popular representative forms, and
other similar institutions, had been prepared in
Prussia, even during the time, of the greatest external oppression, in order to afford the people themselves an opportunity of consulting upon their own
affairs, and to reanimate the public spirit, which
had been so long dormant. Already in the beginning of 1811, the Notables of the nation had been
called together in Berlin, but, under the then existing circumstances, with little benefit to the country; also towards the end of 1813, the representatives of the people ad interim, were summoned, to deliberate upon the equalization of the burthens of the
war, and on the means, of warding off from the
deeply indebted landed-proprietors the necessity of

---

*) Art. 13. — Each of the confederate countries is to
have a constitution, represented by the estates
of the people.

parting with their estates. But the solid foundation of a real popular representation, could not be erected, until after the return of a definitive peace; and the solution of this task, on account of the great claims of the nation, which by reason of the encouragement given to its expectations, can no longer be disregarded, — is looked forward to, with the most longing anxiety. In that part of the former kingdom of Poland, which has come under the dominion of Russia, a national - representation .has been reestablished, approaching the forms of the ancient government. In Sweden, the constitution remained in force, which had been framed, immediately in the beginning of the reign of Charles the thriteenth, after the revolution of the 13th of March 1809, which had placed that monarch on the throne; and it afforded the cooperation of the people in the legislature, at the Diet, greater scope, than they had enjoyed since the act of security of 1789. —

Also in Norway, which, since the treaty of Kiel, of the 14th of Jauuary 1814, has been united with Sweden under one ruler, a representative - constitution, but wholly differing in its forms from that of the latter country, is fully in force. —

Thus it appears, that, since the intoxication of republicanism is evaporated, and military autocracy has been subverted by the too great distension of

its own inherent despotic principles, the universal
tendency of Europe inclines to a legally free constitution, in which the legislative and oeconomical
S'e l f-d e l i b e r a t i o n s of the P e o p l e, are opposed to the elements of M o n a r c h y, a power
irresistably operative in its own sphere, not instituted by virtue of election or by summons, but
having emerged, as it were by the divine will, from
amidst the obscurity of the earliest ages, and not
placed by the side of, but reclining, majestically
supported by itself, above the people. — If the
foundation of the former of these principles origi-
nated in the spirit of the times, and in the just
claims of the people, partly summoned to independance, by their own rulers; the latter one has found
a new support in the Holy Alliance, concluded on
the 15th of Septbr. 1815, which unequivocally declares the relation in which princes, as delegates of
providence, stand to their people, considered as a
family entrusted to their care. It appears from the
above picture, which we have hitherto regularly
sketched out, that a material difference stamps the
character of the European and American state-forms,
the latter acknowledging no other power, bnt what
is delegated, and temporary. —

Nevertheless, there was much wanting, to render Europe unanimous in the approbation of the

principles of its new organization; not even the
distribution of the several countries, can be looked
upon, as definitive; and that sect, which like the
Italian Carbonari *), would wish to deduce the
unity of nation and government, from the unity of
the language, has spread itself far and wide, in more
than one country. The different parties are neither
extirpated, nor dissolved in one another. The destruction of the ancient monarchy; after which, the
overthrow of republicanism; and more latterly the
fall of Buonaparte, have wafted thousands of dis-

*) This order instituted by Murat, for the purpose
    of bringing the whole of Italy under his con-
    troul, and deriving its name from the attach-
    ment shewn by the colliers in Scotland to
    James the IId in his misfortunes; has princi-
    pally brought about the late revolution, of
    the 6th of July, in Naples. — Thus since
    the author published this work, the beginning
    of the present year, two considerable nations, in
    having obtained a constitution, have verified the
    truth of his prophetic ideas; and the late occur-
    rences in Spain and Naples, have at the same
    time shewn, what reliance a sovereign can place
    on a standing army, once animated with the
    sentiments of the people, upholding the inte-
    grity of his power.
                              Translator.

contented (amongst whom are to be found, a great
mass of intelligence, bodily abilities, and considerable
pecuniary resources) to the Western Hemispheres,
where there is scope for every species of activity without collision, for every way of thinking, toleration, with protection and security against secta-
rial hatred, and persecution. The agitated passions,
and the fermentations inseparable from a new order
of things, will still drive many thousands thither,
and thus a part of the existing generation, dissatis-
fied with the present; afraid of taking refuge in the
past; will fly the old world with all its anxieties,
and settle in the new one. They will be cordially
received in those immeasureable regions, where
nature and government yet in happy unison, appear
only to await the diligent comer, in order to bestow
on him, the most desirable of all benefits, a certain subsistence and a dignified free existence, as
the price of a few years of honorable labor and
active perseverance.

VI.

There are still other reasons, independant of the present political state of Europe, which are likely more powerfully to operate, in supplying both Americas with colonists, and in transplanting thither, a share of European cultivation and refinement. It appears namely, that almost every where in the old countries, by the continued developement of an artificial state of society, we have brought it so far, that the quantity of those, whose subsistence does not depend upon the cultivation of the soil, and its attendant employments, or is not founded on some indispensible handicraft, universally necessary, far exceeds the demand for their work or ingenuity. On this account the price of their labor, has been reduced by those for whom they work, much below the limits, which would enable the labourer himself or a family, to enjoy a species of prosperity, and even the produce of some branches of industry, is insufficient for the bare subsistence of life. — The present state of the manufacturing districts of England and Ireland, of Saxony, the provinces on the Rhine, and Swisserland, as well as of France and the Netherlands, sufficiently prove the correctness of the above fact. But as it appears, at first sight, to stand so completely at variance with the encreasing

consumption of manufactures, and the productions
of art, it will not be improper here, to investigate
the subject more closely, should we even be obliged
to be more profuse, than would be judged necessary on a single glance of the matter, in order fully
to illustrate, and account for it. —

The plough was held in the greatest veneration,
amongst all the nations of the ancient world, who
are celebrated in history: the Greek requited the
benefit of those inventions, which transformed the
Nomades into stationary inhabitants, by a place
amongst the Gods, and the Roman fetched his generals from the field, which they were ploughing with
their own hands. Such was not the case with those
Scythian and German tribes, whom the migration
of the nations, seated upon the ruins of the Roman
universal empire *). Amongst them, war alone,
the chace, with every exercise wherein strength and
courage and a contempt of death could be evinced,
were held in esteem. Contending for dominion, and
defending themselves against aggression, constituted

----

*) Agriculturæ non student, says Cæsar, de Bello
Gallico VI, cap. 22, majorque pars victus eorum
lacte et caseo et carne consistit. — Which is
still applicable to the Tartar nations of the present day. —

the acting impulse and occupation of the men; the
women on the other hand took care of house and
field, and under their direction, a little land was
cultivated for the most pressing wants, by the slaves
and bondsmen, who being principally formed of
prisoners of war, and their posterity, became the
ancestors of the later feudal vassals. Christianity
mitigated the severities of slavery; and by a stationary residence, the ancient barbarous manners, wore
gradually off, but still an inclination for contests
and war, has remained predominant, through all
ages, and even at present, according to the reigning
estimation, the profession of arms is undeniably
looked upon as the most honorable state for the free
man, whilst that of agriculture, if it form the immediate occupation of his corporeal exertions, is
considered the most humble. In direct opposition
to the Roman usage, which despised not alone every
handicraft, but the mechanical, and even the fine
arts, which did not depend on oratory, leaving the
profession of such to freedmen and bondsmen, trade,
but still more the arts, were the means of eman-
cipating the slave, amongst the above nations, who
made their appearance in the old Roman territory,
and further to the North and East of Enrope; and
formed in the new cities a respectable and independant class of burghers, who soon militated very pre-
judicially, against the originally-free military estate

(the Nobility). The man of learning stood higher than the citizen, but was however held in slight estimation by the Roman. This antithesis is nevertheless easily to be explained from the nature of the case itself. The barbarians, who inundated the Roman provinces, on viewing the conveniences and ornaments of civilized life, were obliged to respect the workman and the artist, who embellished their existence, and who struck them with admiration, by a fund of intelligence of which the invaders had hitherto, not had the slightest idea. The necessity of maintaining cities, castles and burghs, as fortresses of defence, and the encreasing commercial intercourse which began to exist with the the Orient, by means of the Christian empire at Constantinople, were the causes of the mechanical trades being latterly taken considerably into favor, and new life being given to the arts, which were every where patronized and encouraged, at the courts of princes and within the walls of the monasteries. Thus arose, between the nobility, who were originally free, and the vassal peasant, an intermediate class, with its several gradations, and a restless desire of aspiring to those ranks of society, which possess a pretended preeminence; this eagerness, which shews itself sufficiently active at the present day, receives fresh support, from the privilege of citizens being exempted from forced military service.

With the encreasing population of the cities,
and a further developement of those useful trades,
which attend to the necessities of life, (continually
becoming more numerous) and with the progress of
the mechanical and liberal arts, which are either
generally employed in the improvement and embellishment of our existence, or especially in gratifying
the love of splendor, and the luxury of the powerful and rich, — a number of those also arose, who
drew their support, not immediately from the earth,
but from the price which was paid them for the
supplying of artificial wants; and their numerous
posterity, descended from, and grown up, on this
insecure branch of industry, were confined to these
means of support, under circumstances, wich were
constantly becoming more oppressive. The encreased competition, lessened the price of works perform-
ed by this species of labour; the later generation
lived worse from the same source of emolument than
their progenitors; still more sorrowfully did it supply the wants of the yet more numerous candi-
dates, who followed in the same track, and the exercise of the mechanical crafts have long since ceased
to be peculiarly profitable. For the necessity and
demand for the productions of the mechanic and
the artist, however extensively their consumption
has been encreased, could nevertheless, not remain
in such a proportion with the quantity of workmen,

so as to afford them all a comfortable subsistence, as the fruit of their labor *); more particularly on account of inanimate powers being daily substituted more and more, in the place of human hands, by reason of the rapid progress the mechanical arts have made, and which, independant of the saving of labor, multiply, the quantity of the productions in an equal ratio. Still an equilibrium might have been preserved, as long as productive industry was limited to particular states, which supplied the rest of the world with their manufactures. But since knowledge has been more generally diffused, and the different governments, with a zeal partly erroneous, have endeavored to domesticate every branch of industry, without regard to climate and situation,

----

*) The enormous encrease of paupers receiving alms, and the proportional rise of poor's rates, is to be accounted for particularly by this circumstance. Even Oddy mentions in his European Commerce, published in 1805, that the number of poor receiving alms in England and Wales, constituted nearly an ⅐th part of the whole population, and that the poor's rates which amounted to 5,200,000 Lstg., were double what this tax had been 18 years before. In the year 1819 it had risen to 9,800,000 Lstg.

(12)

and partly through the necessity of employing a
constantly encreasing population, every species of
fabrics and manufactories have been multiplied in
all countries, and men have been drawn into
these branches of trade, whereby — they and their
children for the most part — have been rendered
useless for every other employment. Moreover,
every new invention which by means of an artificial
power, renders the use of hands superfluous, will produce a surplus of those seeking employment, and will
thereby lower the wages of those, who are still fortunate enough to find work, to the most scanty pittance.

It will not do to say, that there is more soil,
than the hand of man is capable of cultivating, and
that the advancement of the spirit of human invention, will always open new canals for unoccupied
vigor to flow into. It must be taken first into
consideration here, that men, thrust by necessity out of their own sphere, are not so easily accommodated in a new one, and that ancient customs,
and the direction once given to the mind and the
body, will much rather maintain their rights.
Take a certain number of families of silk or cloth-
weavers, of iron or steel manufacturers, deprived of
work, and let us see, how they or their children
already accustomed to their trades, would be suitable
for other employments. — The nature of the thing
and experience shew the contrary; they would en-

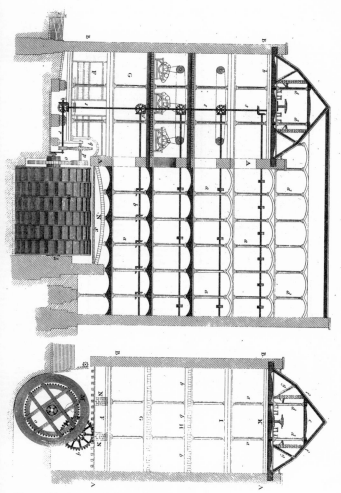

The rapid progress of the mechanical arts

Negroes washing for diamonds in Brazil

crease the poor-lists, or become sharpers and vaga-
bonds, provided a war did not offer a part of them an
opportunity of enlisting and being destroyed. Moreover the institutions of guilds, privileges, and mono-
polies, of all descriptions, render the entrance into
a new trade, difficult every where, if not impossible,
and when we tell the idle man, to go and cultivate
the earth, we must remember, that the soil of every
country, where such superfluity of human hands
exists, is already occupied, although it may not be
tilled, and that new lands are difficult to be obtained, and more difficult to be brought under the
plough. — Neither ought we to forget, that the improvement of the mechanical powers, has also been
extended to agriculture, and that the new - invented
plough, the threshing and sowing - machines, and
other implements used in husbandry, save many
hands, and promise for the future to dispense with
many more; and that, the cultivation of the earth
has become reduced to such scientific principles, (if
we may be allowed the expression), as to render it
day by day, more difficult for those, who have not
been brought up to it from their youth. — We may
therefore with justice presume, that multitudes of
the indigent and unemployed, will emigrate to the
Western continent, particularly if our quarter of
the globe be not visited by war and sickness; and
the cow-pox continue to shield the infant from

death, and be the means of encreasing population.
For it is the interest of America to domesticate natural
industry, and the mechanical arts and trades, within herself, and thus become independant of all
supplies from Europe; and it is here, that mere physical strength alone, without any given tendency,
or studied activity, finds employment and superfluous support, in the primitive cultivation of a soil
never before tilled by the hand of man, or in the
erection of habitations on places hitherto occupied
by eternal forests. —

If we at length turn our view, to the present
state of agriculture in many countries of Europe,
it will appear evident that even the paternal soil, in
many districts, is becoming too confined, to afford
nourishment for those, who have remained faithful
to it. If in mountainous countries, as for example
in the West and South of France, on the Alps, and
along the Rhine, every spot is employed, and the
very earth and manure have for centuries been carried aloft upon the naked rock, attended with the
most boundless labor, in order to furnish soil for the
vine, the olive, or for the different species of cerea-
lia, and at present no further room exists for a more
extended cultivation; it is not possible for a more
numerous growing generation to find nourishment
in these districts, whose productions are incapable
of an encreased progression. The too frequent prac-

tice of parcelling out common-lands and large estates, a principle originally beneficial in itself, has
effected a similar thing in other states. It was
undoubtedly a wise and humane plan, to transform
commons and extensive pastures into fruitful fields,
and by dividing large estates, which their owners
could not overlook, into smaller lots, ensure more
abundant crops, and an encrease of population, by
a more careful cultivation of them. But if, as is
already the case at the present day, in several parts,
useful lands have been split into so many small
independant possessions, as to render it hardly possible for families occupying such very inconsiderable
lots of land, to subsist in the most penurious manner by the cultivation of them, whence then, is sustenance to be obtained for the more numerous posterity, and from what is the state to derive its taxes?
It is evident, that this condition of things, must
lead to the most poignant distress, and that a bread-
less multitude, either driven by irretrievable debts
from their paternal huts, or voluntarily forsaking
them, on account of an inadequate maintenance,
will turn their backs upon their homes, and it may
be considered the most fortunate resource, if they,
as has frequently occurred in the later times, carry
with them, the vigor of their strength, to the free
states of America, which stand in need of no one

thing, but human hands, rapidly to raise them to the highest degree of prosperity *). And those governments under which, such an unnatural distension of the state of society prevails, ought not most assuredly for their own advantage, and for the sake of humanity, by any means, to throw obstacles in the way of, or prevent, but favor such emigration, and render it easy and consolatory for all, since they have it not in their power to offer a better remedy for their present misery. By doing this, they will prevent dangerous ebullitions, and unruly disaffections of an overgrown population; they will lighten the number of their poor, which are encreasing to a most alarming extent, and will put an end to the crying state of abjectness and misery, which is felt by every honest heart, and to which so many thousands are sunk down, who with numerous families in hovels of squallidness, prolong their

---

*) As this relates to the state of things, as they are at present, and as they are likely to remain for the first, we shall on the other hand, endeavor to shew in the Xth chapter how Europe, under different circumstances at a future time, will be able to support, improve, and employ her population in an honorable way. —

corporeal existence, more scantily, than the most
domestic animals, and who appear only to be gifted
with spiritual feelings, in order to be more sensible
of their forlorn and pitiable fate. Or shall history,
then, this book of instruction and warning eternally
before our eyes, ever remain a dead letter, and never, as a living oracle, bring forth wise determinations and fresh laudable actions? And does it not
teach us, how the people of the ancient world freed
themselves, from their fermenting elements, how
Greeks-and Romans founded colonies in distant parts,
enlivened deserts by commercial establishments,
and transplanted the treasures, of art, of life, and
refined manners to the wild barbarian? How the
Germans, the forefathers of the Northern-Euro-
peans, sent forth their swarms of younger population, their ver sacrum? —

That a noble minded German, — for who can
deny Gagern this appellation? — has seriously in-
terested himsslf for this most important cause, and
has illumined the path, which so many must yet
tread, — cannot but belong to the many improve-
ments, which the latest times have brought to light;
as also, that the Swiss government at Freiburg has
been the first, — which, with due consideration,
and a laudable care, has by formal treaties, attended

to the future welfare and fate of their countrymen, who mean to erect their huts in Brazil *).

VII.

After the foregoing discussion, we may take it for granted, that the free states of North America,

----

*) The author is well aware, that many emigrants, particularly in the later times to North - America, have not alone been disappointed in not meeting with the ease and affluence they expected, but have been unable to gain a mere sustenance; — but this proves nothing againt the principle itself. Every person is not fit for emigration, and those who are suitable for it, have not always, nay seldom, gone the right way and methodically to work. Gagern's work "The German in North America", shews most forcibly, who should emigrate; and how and by what means he can and must gain a livelihood, and attain future prosperity. According to the latest accounts, the Swiss colony in Brazil, appears to be in a thriving condition.

will encrease in population, more rapidly, than any other territory, partly on account of emigrations from Europe, and partly in consequence of the acknowledged laws of population, on large tracts of land lately brought under cultivation. —

But this end will also materially be forwarded by the salutary effects of an almost universal prosperity or well-being, which keeps at a distance, every mean oppression, filthy penury, hunger and those diseases arising from scanty nourishment and crowded habitations; all which tend to depress the growth and the chearful thriving of the younger generation in those states, where children are no longer a blessing of heaven, but oftner a burthen, which brings their indigent parents and protectors to ruin. — It is natural to suppose, that the encrease of population, the extended cultivation of the soil, and the multiplied sources of sustenance and of trade, will first lead to the cherishment of the technical and afterwards of the fine arts, as well as the abstract and useful sciences. We dare further assert, that the influence of their free form of government, will continually develope more happily in the new people, the features of indepenednce, and that intelligence, which is animated, and receives the greater stimulus, the less constraint the human faculties labour under. As the developement of no

(13)

power ever remains stationary, as long as no adequate counterpoise be opposed to it, it would not be
too bold to advance, that the European colonies in
the North-Eastern parts of America will follow the
general impulse, and as, has lately been the case
with both the Floridas, will unite themselves with
the other independent states. —

With the same degree of probability, the observer can foresee the event of the conflict which has
commenced in Spanish America, as well on
this, as on the other side of the isthmus of Darien.
— Nature ever asserts her right, and this is, that
the colony, at a state of majority will throw off its
guardianship and will not derive its laws from the
other side of the Ocean, but will form them within
itself, and will promulgate them internally over its
whole proper independent territory. Without wishing to determine the period, or the ways and means,
when and by which, the independence of these
countries, the richest and most blessed by nature,
of the whole globe, will shine forth in all its lustre,
we have, following the course of events, considered
it as an occurrence, which must infallibly take place,
sooner or later; and which will be particularly
favored by external and internal influence of every
description; having already at its commencement,
allured over a number of fiery heads and daring

adventurers, who could find no room on the confined and limited stage of European affairs. —

Without therefore for the present entering into
deeper discussions, we adopt the supposition, as the
basis of our enquiries: that the whole of America,
to the North and South of the Isthmus, has become
independent of Europe, and been formed into states,
governed by their own laws, and that the West-India islands, following the example of the continent
laying nearest to them, have torn themselves from the
European mother countries, and now ask: W h a t
w i l l   b e   t h e   e f f e c t s   o f   s u c h   a   c h a n g e
u p o n   t h e   c i v i l i z e d   w o r l d   i n   a l l   i t s   d i f -
f e r e n t   p a r t s ,   a n d   w h a t   i n f l u e n c e   s u c h
a   r e v o l u t i o n   o f   t h e   o r d e r   o f   t h i n g s   i s
l i k e l y   t o   h a v e   u p o n   A s i a   a n d   A f r i c a ,
b e i n g   t h o s e   p a r t s   o f   t h e   g l o b e ,   w h i c h
s t a n d   a t   p r e s e n t   u p o n   t h e   l o w e s t   s t e p
o f   c u l t i v a t i o n ? —

We are well aware, that in order to have taken
our subject in its greatest compass, we ought to have
placed the question thus: what will be the situation
of the civilized world, on the C o l o n i a l - s y s t e m,
wholly having ceased, by reason of the emancipation of all the European dependencies? But placed
in this manner, the enquiry would lead into too
great lengths, which would not rest upon the base
of actual occurrences, and after having first succeeded

in having developed with some degree of clearness
the consequences of the approaching revolution, and
on the actual results of such having in the sequel,
shewn the justness or nullity of our conjectures,
some later enquirers, might be bold enough to cast
a look to a more distant period; and the first result
which would perhaps offer itself to their view,
would be, that the independence of America in the
above extended sense, must necessarily carry with
it, the total overthrow of the whole colonial-system.

The consequences of the discovery and colonization of America, remodelled Europe, and her
emancipation will in like manner once more, entirely alter the form of the latter.   This is the first
proposition, which we have to unfold; we ground
it on the assertion, that, Europe, continuing to
exist in her present shape, cannot do, without America; but that this deprivation inevitably awaits her,
as a necessary consequence of the emancipation of
the new continent; whereas America on the other
hand, has no occasion for Europe, and her communication with the latter in the reciprocal way of
trade must necessarily cease.   We dedicate the next
chapter to the consideration of this idea. —

VIII.

Europe cannot exist without America, shall she remain, as she is at present; for the European was centuries ago, and continues to be, monarch of the terrestrial globe, sovereign by the superiority of his intelligence, by the extent of his external possessions, by the produce of his still more extended commerce, and by the tribute, which he attracts to himself, from every corner of the earth, of all the splendid treasures, which inanimate nature can boast of, and of all what the industry of millions of beings, working only for his purpose, can accomplish. — Agreable to this spirit of sovereignty, the passion for dominion has formed itself, which characterizes the European above all other people, and which, although kept within bounds at home by an universal claim to such pretensions, immediately bursts forth, as soon as He has passed the pillars of Hercules, ploughing the ocean to the West or the South, to assert and maintain his preminence, on the remotest shores. — Wrapped up in this sense of royalty, he reclines at home, shining in borrowed splendor and majesty, derived from the produce of every distant region, which lustre, his own resources, would never have been able to invest him with; he continues revelling in enjoyments, which nature has denied him, accustomed from his most tender youth to wants, which all the blessings and donations of the land and the ocean, produced within the compass of his own quarter of the globe, are unable to satisfy; and above all, often unmindful of, and despising the treasures and useful elements, which his paternal soil, so abundantly contains within its bosom. Every one will be sensible of, by his own manner of living, that this picture is not too highly colored, and the observer, acquainted with Europe generally, and in detail, from the palace of the prince to the retreat of poverty, will upon the whole confirm the truth of our assertion. —

The precious metals, which, by an inherent value, of all the productions of nature, alone unite those properties in themselves, which a circulating medium, destined to determine the price of labor between man and man, ought to possess, in order to answer this end, have only, since the working of the American mines, flowed into the different channels of circulation, in such quantities, as to have rendered it possible, for the commerce of the world to have become so extended; and for industry, founded on a sagacious attention to the improvement of the mechanical arts, particularly in Britain, to have attained its present height, which principally constitute the superiority of Europe. — If she is to retain this ascendancy, the quantity of gold and silver flowing to her, must not be diminished; nay, it must rather be encreased, to be able only to maintain the present order of things, by averting and destroying, that intolerable number of representative means of payment (truer, non-valeurs), which a constantly encreasing population, in a state of society more and more complicated, for reciprocal services and occasions, and the unproductive expenditure of capitals wasted in imaginary national-wants, have brought to light, and the burthen of which apparently seems to threaten to burst asunder, all the ties of civilized life. — The spoils of the new world, in like manner first occasioned the present extensive use of jewels, and the precious metals; which being wrought into useful utensils and rich implements, or appropriated to the embellishment of articles of luxury, in furniture or apparel, afford employment and support to a numerous class of artificers. —

But America, has not alone furnished in a degree unknown in former times, the means of an intercourse, upon the basis of which, the existing relation of the different classes and the whole concatenation of the civil institutions of society in general, have been formed, and retained to the present day; nor has she furnished us alone with the elements of a more modern splendor and a more sumptuous magnificence, but also other gifts received from thence, have changed the whole features of social life. The costly descriptions of timber, which South America, and the Bahama Islands produce, have supplanted the use of inland woods for the purposes of furniture and implements in the houses of the rich; instead of madder has cochineal, and instead of woad has indigo become an actual necessity of the better classes. Rice, an article of nourishment, now generally made use of in the most humble families, is a gift of the Western Continent, scarcely to be replaced by any other substitute *); Cotton, tobacco, coffee, sugar, molasses and rum, these staple-articles of the larger Antilles and the American continent, although more doubtful as to their actual worth, have nevertheless universally become necessaries, incapable of being supplanted. In comparison with the above articles, the consumption of cocoa certainly appears more inconsiderable, nevertheless chocolade, seasoned with Mexican and Peruvian vanilla, is a necessity for the Spaniard and Italian, and an article of luxury in the North of

---

*) The potatoe and Maize or Turkish corn, are not mentioned here, on account of these vegetables having become so indigenous in Europe, as to render it longer unnecessary to import them from their native country.

Europe; the numerous and precious drugs, which
the Western continent furnishes us with, are, according to the newest system of medicinal science, to
be termed truly indispensible necessaries; the trade
in Vigonia wool, furs, and other articles principally within the reach of the opulent alone, are less
worthy of notice.

The greater the consequence is, for the continuation of the European state and civil-existence,
by procuring these supplies, grown absolutely necessary by long habit, and by the powerful efforts
of the lower classes, universally striving to attain
the advantages and enjoyments of the higher orders,
the more unfavorable is it, for our continent, that
the above articles cannot be domesticated either
at all, with us, or in that degree, so as to render
their cultivation productive of advantage; for Europe is deficient in warmth and in the other properties of the tropic climates. We do not take into account here, that rice is cultivated to advantage in
some few parts of Lombardy, in Sicily and the Io-
nian islands, where a considerable quantity of sugar
likewise grows, or that a part of the demand might
be supplied from the neighboring Egypt. If the
existing European mode of life is to continue, America will perpetually supply the grand bulk of our
wants. On the other hand, the decided preponde-

(14)

rance of America, consists in the present undoubted, and for the future incalculable advantage, that all the natural productions, which Europe has transplanted thither, in return for such noble presents, have become indigenous, not in inconsiderable districts merely for trial, but universally so, and capable of fully supplying the present and every future want; and that those European productions, which now only go thither in the way of trade, can, and shortly will also become indigenous there, on the American colonial relation to Europe having ceased.

The horse, unknown on the new continent, prior to the Spanish occupation of it, is become the domestic animal, mostly used for the carriage and the plough in North, and in South America having again assumed its native wildness, ranges over her boundless plains; but on being once more subjected to the bridle, it has trained in the interior of Chili and Peru, powerful tribes of intrepid Indians, to an Arabian course of life and art of war. Although the use of lactiferous animals, was unknown in the ancient kingdom of the Aztecks, in the territories of the Peruvian Inkas, or much less amongst the hunting tribes of Brazil, the ox, is found every where at present, either as a domestic animal, affording nourishment, or in a state of nature; and Buenos Ayres supplies Europe with hides of an un-

Ox hunting in Brazil, north of Rio de Janeiro

Barclay's Iron Works in Saugerties on the Hudson River, United States

common size and beauty, which the descendants of
European breeds, invigorated by their wild condition, are obliged to offer up at the shrine of commerce. Of the different discriptions of European
bread-corn, nature had only furnished America
with maize; they are all now, universally grown
there; oats are produced in the smallest quantity,
rye and barley in greater proportion, but wheat
most abundantly, which returns on an average, in
the North of Mexico, for one seed of corn 17 and
in the South 24, on the river Plate 12, whereas in
the luxuriant France, and in the North of Germany, 5 to 6 corn upon one of seed are generally calculated upon. The cultivation of the European vine,
(Vitis vinifera) — has commenced with success in
Virginia, and in the Swiss colony of New-Vevay on
the Ohio, and has florished long in Mexico; it will
become general, and adequate for every demand,
as soon as it is not limited by considerations of
trade with European mother countries, and as soon
as the encreasing population supplies more hands
for the tillage of the soil. According to Humboldt's
respectable testimony *), the same is the case with
the olive, which thrives admirably in several plantations of New Spain, but the cultivation of which,

---

*) Humboldt. Essai politique I. p. 304.

the mother - country has purposely prevented, in
order to retain the monopoly of the supply of European oil. The new world could also long since have
produced its silk, from its own soil; for Cortez
free from little considerations, and looking into
futurity with the view 'of a true statesman, had
already introduced the European mulberry - tree and
the silk worm into Mexico; but the jealous policy
of the Spanish government, has industriously
thrown obstacles in the way, to depress the rise of
this branch of industry, as well as the breeding of
the indigenous silk - worm *), upon the same principle, that the Dutch formerly prevented the propagation of the spice-plants, and destroyed half the
produce of rich crops, in order to keep the goods up
at a higher market price. — The sheep which were
imported long since from Spain, produce a wool neither inferior in length, fineness, nor softness to the
best European; but the breeding of them is inconsiderable, except in the Viceroyalty of Plata, but

---

*) In Mexico, there is an indigenous silkworm,
different from that of the mulberry tree, from
the web of which, pocket-handkerchiefs are wo-
ven in the Intendancy of Oxaca,. which possess a
roughness in the feeling, similar to that of certain East India silks, and which they first lose,
on being used some time,

can be extended on the continent, as also on the Antilles, at pleasure. On the Isthmus of Yucatan large quantities of wax are collected from an indigenous species of bee, having no sting, and on the opposite island of Cuba, about Havannah; the culture of the European bee (Apis mellifica) which has been transplanted thither, has already become very general; in the flowery vallies of Mexico, this branch of-industry being more cultivated, will rapidly encrease, and furnish adequate supplies of honey and wax. Canada, the two Carolinas, and New-Spain, have a superfluity of flax and hemp, timber for building ships, and the golden fruits of the Hesperian gardens are of equal goodness, and in greater quantity, in the tropic-districts of America, than in the southern countries of Europe, which are washed by the Mediterranean sea. Nature has moreover so lavishly endowed this favored portion of the globe, with vegetables, that they far surpass those brought thither from Europe, in point of nourishment. The Banana-tree, the Manioc root, maize and the potatoe would alone be sufficient, to banish all idea of want of articles of sustenance, and of dependance upon foreign supplies, even without the European descriptions of grain; and even deprived of the European vine, the Agave would supply the American, with an agreable vinous liquor *). Neither is the new continent, abounding so lavishly in the precious metals, deficient in a single useful one, of the inferior descriptions; near her gold mines in Brazil, whole chains of mountains have been discovered full of iron-stone, which is already being worked by German industry; a more careful attention to the quicksilver veins in Mexico, will render all supply of Idria from hence, superfluous for the future. Copper and tin, won from the mountains in the interior of Plata, will be supplied from Buenos Ayres; San Domingo, above all the Antilles, is particularly rich in coal, tin, lead, marble and porphyry.

America, thus standing in need of none of the European natural productions, but rather possessing within herself, more nnmerous and more precious gifts of nature, than any other quarter of the globe, will also be able to dispense with the works of foreign industry and art, as soon as she can command,

---

*) America will even require far less supplies of tea, when the leaves of the Paraguayan tea-plant which are said to be equally strong of flavor & as palatable to the taste, as the Chinese, come more generally, into use. The cultivation of the Chinese tea-plant has also been attempted with success in Brazil.

the necessary stock of knowledge, and a sufficient
number of industrious hands, which she will soon
find at her disposal, partly by the emigration of
artificers from Europe, and partly by her own encreasing population, who will become versed in the arts,
which are introduced amongst them. Where there
exists matter, and understanding to use it, the freedom of handling the whole at pleasure, and security
in the enjoyment of the fruits of labor, the spirit
of enterprize is called into life, and with it florishes
every branch of human industry. If hitherto the
leading influence of the mother-countries turned
the industry of their colonies, to the cultivation of
the so-called colonial-articles, which promised an
advantageous sale in Europe, and forbid or at least
rendered difficult, the exercise of those descriptions
of agronomic, ingenious, and mechanical employments, the produce of which, an exclusive system
of trade had reserved to itself, to supply, activity
will on the other hand, soon take a different direction, on the attainment of political emancipation,
an occurrence, which we have taken for granted
will happen. The attention to the defence and maintenance of independence, alone brings life into a
multitude of employments relating to warfare by
land or by sea. The soldier must be clothed, appointed with arms and horses, with ammunition and
heavy ordnance, and a thousand considerable and

lesser field-requisites, which imperative necessity, soon points out the way of furnishing and fabricating on the spot. The coasts must be covered by armed vessels, large and smaller ships of war must be built, masts, cordage, sail-cloth, pitch, tar and an infinite number of articles necessary for the fitting out and keeping a squadron at sea, must be made and supplied: all which were never once thought of, during the colonial relationship; alone affording a vast number of hands occupation and support, and which are the means of quickly diffusing, and bringing the exercise of many of the mechanical arts, into constant practice. This was the case with North America, who, at the commencement of her revolution, found herself nearly destitute, of all technical resources and means of defence; whereas now, she is in possession of considerable fortifications, and stores of ammunition; has already formed a spirited and daily growing navy, and is complete mistress of the different branches of knowledge, and contains all those mechanical institutions, requisite for the encrease and maintenance of these things. Similar efforts are now making in South America for public independence, and they will, — should the attempts succeed — bring forth similar results. But little does the independence of a country avail, or at least insecure is its foundation, if the united members of such state, be obliged to procure their means of subsistence, as well as the articles of daily consumption, from abroad, and cannot do without such. Therefore, as soon as North-America began her conflict for liberty, her government and her inhabitants acted upon the principle; that in order to be truly independent, a state must be capable of finding within itself, every thing requisite for its maintenance and wants in the most extended sense, without being obliged to have recourse to foreign countries for these. Under the influence of this spirit, fabrics and manufactories quickly arose, which supplied the most important articles of consumption, undoubtedly of rough texture, and coarse stuffs, but nevertheless sufficiently good, for a people neither spoiled, nor difficult in their choice, who had a sublimer object in view, than physical welfare. Thus the first seed was quickly sown in the enthusiasm of the moment; and although since peace has been restored, luxury has shewn the preference to European, and more particularly to British manufactures, whereby many establishments of the above nature, have been thrown aside as not mature, and have been obliged to give way to the occupations of agriculture, fisheries, and trade, yet the ground-work of mechanical skill and ingenuity, as well as the actual exercise of those trades and arts, which were able to supply the

coarser necessities of life in a taste nòt too offensive,
have taken root. The commencement will also be
made with the finer articles of consumption, as soon
as the advanced state of the cultivation of the soil,
which manufacturing industry must ever follow, but
qn no account precede, yields a superfluous quantity of hands; and the emigration from abroad, and
the encrease of internal population, naturally lowering the disproportionate price of labor in America, at a time perhaps that the same will be raised
in Europe, (which cannot but take place in the
long-run) will alter the circumstances, under which
the American manufacturer works, and be the means
of bringing his productions more upon a par, with
those of the old world. For hitherto, the most European goods, can be imported cheaper from across
the Atlantic, than if fabricated on the spot. The
American government, has notwithstanding acted
here very wisely, in not having interfered with prohibitory laws of importation, and restrictive edicts,
as a certain intelligent and acute traveller, formerly wished *); but in having let the thing take

----

*) Voyage dans les Etats Unis d'Amérique fait en
1795, 1796 and 1797 par la Rochefoucald-Lian-
court; Tome 8me à Paris l'an VII. de la répub-
lique pag. 4. sqq.

its natural course, which first allows fabrics and
manufactories to flourish, when capital can no longer be placed more advantageously in land, when
the raw productions are at hand, and as cheap, as in
other foreign rival states, and when there is a sufficient number of idle hands, who can be profitably
employed in these branches of industry. The same
course, which, by a wise administration, things
must equally take in South America, where already
the most sources of oeconomy are not unknown, but
even considerable progress made in them *), will

---

*) Besides the working of the mines, and the me-
chanical employments dependent thereon, gold
and silver, as also curious carved work in ivory
and wood, is executed in Spanish America; and
it is of great importance for the time to come, that Mexico, as well as Peru and Chili,
possess in their natives, a population, industrious
like the Chinese, and legally free, whose natural dispositions, may be easily adapted to the
ingenious exercise of many useful mechanical arts.
For the innate G r a n d e z z a of the European
predominant race, will for the first, only con-
descend to superintend and direct the fabrics
and manufactories, but will deter it for a long
time, from participating in the labor itself, as
beneath its dignity. Agriculture alone, however,
makes a rare exception in Peru and Chili; being

undoubtedly, render America, in a much shorter period, than is generally supposed capable of not only
dispensing with European manufactures, but of supplying even in the first place, the West-India islands, where the growth of plantations is likely
ever to remain the principal object, with the productions of her fabrics and arts. Here we must on no
account lose sight of the most important circumstance, that the great rivers and lakes, in which
America so considerably surpasses the other parts of
the globe, as far as our knowledge of them goes —
for regarding the interior of Africa, no satisfactory
account has hitherto been given — profusesy offer
the means of an inland communication, which renders uncommon facilities to the rapid circulation of
every production of industry and nature from the
remotest parts. This very animated internal intercourse, on such an extensive territory, must render
foreign trade eventually more and more superfluous,

----

otherwise principally exercised by Negroes, Mu-
lattos, and Indians. In Brazil the presence of
the court, has had very beneficial effects in this
respect; there are at present sail cloth manufactories, cotton spinneries and fabrics in metal, in
a most thriving condition there. In la Plata the
manufacture of woollens for home consumption
and the neigboring Peru, is entered upon.

particularly since the invention of steam-boats, of which such manifold use has already been made in North-America, and which offer facilities, never before known, of navigating rivers and streams. On the immense and arid plains of Terra Firma, the more extensive propagation af the camel, which is already introduced in the Caraccas, seems on the other hand to afford the possibility of caravans, which can become of the greatest importance for reciprocal communication between the two continents, over the isthmus of Panama.

The foregoing investigation, seems indoubtedly to prove, that America, including the West-India Islands, considered as independent, can and will do entirely without Europe. It is not our province to determine, when such an event will take place; it is sufficient, that the natural course of things warrants its happening once, although perhaps after infinite toil, and a determined opposition on the part of European jealousy. But on its having occurred, what will be the consequences thereof in the first place for Europe, and then for the rest of the world? —

IX.

Europe pays her present consumption of West-India and American goods, with some productions of nature, but principally with those of her fabrics and manufactories, which the American particularly values, and imports in considerable quantities. Two cases only are possible, when America, as has been shewn, is once enabled to supply herself with these articles. The European must either procure new markets for the consumption of his wines and oils, for his linens, shawls, hats, leather, iron, glass and fancy-wares, and with the value of these, pay for the American produce, as he at present pays for tea, and other Chinese or East-India goods; or a renunciation must be made of that, which is no longer to be acquired and obtained, and Europe must abdicate the throne of the world, on which nature has not ordained her to sit eternally. After the emigration of those, who may not be reconciled to the new order of things, she must, retiring within herself, endeavor to regain from her own soil, and her adjacent dependences, by internal application, what she has suffered in external splendor, and foreign enjoyments. We will in the first place take a nearer view, of the former of these alternatives. —

Suppose we even were to lose America, it may be answered; Europe still retains her extensive East-India kingdom, her Molucca islands, her numerous establishments on the coasts of Africa, her colonies on the islands of the South Sea, her commercial connexion with China, with the Levant, with Arabia, Ægypt and the coasts of Barbary. She will be enabled by the sale of the productions of her arts and manufactures, to procure her rice and cotton from Bengal, her coffee from Arabia, Bourbon, Isle de France, and Madagascar; her sugar from Ægypt, from the African dependencies, and from the favored island of Otaheitie; her silver from her own mines, worked more attentively, and the gold she has occasion for, from the rivers and sands of Africa. Provided the European only retain the superiority of his intelligence with his spirit of enterprize, colonies will arise, in deserts now occupied by wandering hords of barbarians; and Asia and Africa, under European management, will perhaps deposit richer treasures at the feet of the monarch of the earth, than the new continent formerly did. Moreover the commercial intercourse of America with Europe, will never be broken off suddenly, and whilst the ancient channels are gradually closing up, the ever restless spirit of speculation, will long before, have opened new sources of emolument.

We allow, that the expected change will not take place suddenly, without gradual transitions, and we admit further, that industry in the new Columbian states, will first be directed principally to the bringing agriculture and the working of the mines to perfection. But as far as regards North America, it must be remembered, that several, particularly the Atlantic states, have attained, during the forty three years of their independence, that state of culture and population, as to be able to supply some workmen and encouragement sufficient, for the establishment of fabrics and manufactories, and that the encreasing emigration of artificers from Europe, who are no longer capable of finding support there, must necessarily hasten the period, when the price of labor — at present the principal obstacle to more rapid progress — must fall, on account of greater competition. There is already a considerable surplus of naval stores, train-oil, tallow spermaceti aud candles for exportation; tanneries are every where in the original United states, in the most flourishing condition, and instead of the former importation of shoes and boots, many hundred thousand pair are now annually shipped. Thus every such triumph of internal industry, appropriates to itself, a branch of European emolument, and consolidates the oeconomical independence of the Union. But the complete emancipation of Spanish and the other parts of South America, is likely to have more rapid and more extensive consequences, than that of North America, in as much, as, by its operations, the exportation of silver and gold which is annually made from thence to Europe, and which Humboldt reckons to be about 35 millions of piastres *), must for the greatest part, or wholly cease. For this mass of precious metals did not come to Europe, exclusively in the ordinary course of trade, in exchange for her productions, or as payment for the surplus of a balance of commerce disadvantageous to America. It was sent for the most part, thither, as actual tribute, which the mother-countries drew from their colonies, and which flowed either into the treasuries of the crowns of Spain and Portugal, to whom, besides the gain of their private domains, an aliquot part **) of the net produce of all private mines, as a feodal tythe, belonged, or was forwarded to the large landed proprietors, amongst whom the districts abounding in minerals

---

*) Essai politique Tome IV. pag, 259.

**) In the beginning ½th, afterwards, on mining becoming more difficult and more expensive ¹⁄₁₀th, but on Brazil gold the original ⅕th part is levied.

had been divided since the conquest, or it was secretly introduced into Europe by private persons, who had been able to enrich themselves clandestinely in the mines *). It lays in the nature of the case, that this wealth, which arrived annually at stated periods in the Western peninsula, finding no employment there, flowed in a thousand channels to those states, which worked for the Spaniard, whose majestic inactivity is averse to labour, and spread itself further over the North - eastern countries of Europe, in exchange for raw productions, the true aliments of industry; but, as soon as all the ties of dependency on the old world are severed for ever, these treasures must remain in their native regions **).

---

*) Fischer asserts in his latest description of Brazil, that the Portuguese Government is at least defrauded of a fourth part of the gold that is found, and that it scarcely receives the half of the diamonds which are discovered, and which wholly belong to the crown.

**) That this failure in the supplies of bullion, has already taken place, in a degree very sensibly felt by the trade and monied system of Europe, is proved by an article of the 15th June 1819 in the Börsenhalle newspaper, which states, that instead of 24 Millions of dollars, as formerly, from 1811 to 1818 only 8,111115 dollars have been annual-

But the immediate consequence of this must be, that the quantity of industry, which was paid and maintained in Europe, by these annual supplies of specie, must, by their failure, become stagnant, and the mass of raw productions which was furnished by one, and manufactured by another part of our quarter of the globe, so intimately connected together by these very precious metals since the discovery of America, will become superfluous. Whereas on the other hand, these treasures which for the future will remain in America, must be the means of animating the same mass of industry there, and of supplying an equal quantity of raw productions, and manufactures; whereby however, the epocha of the revolution of the existing order of things in Europe, will more quickly be brought about, than its reestablishment can possibly be accomplished by virtue of any other substituted resources.

For Europe, to be able to dispense with the intercourse with America, and the vent she has hitherto enjoyed for her productions there, and still to continue to exist in the accustomed abundance, must not alone have it in her power to retain in their

---

ly imported into Europe from Mexico. — Since the arrival of the court in Brazil, no bullion is allowed to be exported from thence.

fullest integrity, the remaining branches of the commerce of the world, but she must be able to extend and render them more beneficial; she must enter into new connexions, and colonize territories, which have hitherto remained inaccessible to her, in order that a new colonial system of dominion arise from the ruins of the old one, capable of making amends for what was lost, and of giving fresh life to declining industry. But the necessary energy, appears to be wanting for either of these measures, and in those quarters, where such might be applied with a probability of success, she will have to encounter the competition of America, powerful even at present, and probably in a short time, decisively preponderant. The ancient colonial and commercial system of Europe was founded upon the precious metals of the new world, and the monopoly of navigation, and of every production of art and trade; it continually reposed on these pillars, and without them, will not be able to support itself. As soon as the importation of silver into Europe, ceases, which already has begun to be the case, she must give up the trade to China and Japan, which is carried on, principally by means of bullion, and which will be then prosecuted much nearer across the Pacific from Monterey, Acapulko, Lima, La Conception, and even from Brazil, round Cape Horn. The Chinese and the Japanese, are also likely to be on more friendly terms, with the downright trading American, than with the European, whose constant striving after dominion, they dread, and whose zeal for proselyting (subservient only to a cunning commercial policy) they detest and abhor. — The state of European affairs in the East Indies, is well known; the fire which Hyder Ali, Tippo Saib, Holkar and Scindiah lighted up, continues inextinguishably to glow under a very superficial layer of ashes; and although the deposition of the latter unfortunate Mahratta prince, and the subjugation of his states, apparently completed, by the Marquis of Hastings, have once more extended, and rendered the British empire in India, for the present secure, yet, the resentment in the minds of the natives, has been the more rancorously encreased, and will be continually kept in partial eruptions, by the minor warfare of the Seiks and Pindharris. The mischievous principle of founding a state on the commerce of a distant part of the world, and raising a company of English merchants, to be regents of a territory, at least fifteen-times as large as the mother country, including Ireland, and containing a population of five-times as many inhabitants *), has

---

*) The English territory proper, in the East Indies, according to William Playfair's calculations,

depressed the trade of the company for a long time
back, by the weight of an expensive administration ;
on the other hand, the spirit of trade inherent in
the new sovereigns, and the mean rapaciousness of
their servants, but badly kept in check, have been
the means of forming a system of government, which
preys upon the vitals of the state, if it may be termed such. The ¡lasting D u r a t i o n of such an organization, which endeavors to unite complete heterogeneous elements — as the art of government
and the procecution of commerce — is scarcely possible, and the encrease of a real surplus gain for Europe by means of it, is still less imaginable. The
financial state of the British company, which has
only been successful in preventing other European
competition, has in the lapse of time been conside-

---

contained, before the last conquests 217,185 square
English miles, but the tributary states, governed
in fact by the company, but administered by its
vassals, consisted of 235,467, together 452,652
square miles. The subjugated Mahratta state
contains, according to the same author, 447,144
thus making in the whole, 899,796 square miles.
He estimates the population of the ancient territory at 23,057300, of that which is tributary,
at 17,995590, and of the Mahratta states, at
28,342928, together 69,395818 souls.

rably impaired *); and the fear is not groundless, which many entertain, that either an insurrection of the Indian nations, fed by the commercial jea-lousy of other powers, will one day overthrow this merchant-kingdom, or that an independent throne, founded by Europeans in India, around which, under a mild government, the gentle and docile native people, would willingly flock, will put an end to transatlantic supremacy and mercantile extor-tions. In trade, America has already very success-fully entered the lists **). For whilst, in Spanish America, the intercourse with ancient India, has been limited and is monopolized by Akapulko, the United states, are in the habit of sending annually a considerable number of vessels, to East India ports,

---

*) According to official accounts, the debt of the East India Company in India, amounted in the beginning of 1819 to 34,184137 Lstg. at 6, 8 and 9 pro cent interest. Fullarton's celebrated work; A view of the English interests in India, gives such disclosures as to the administration of Eri-tish India, as completely to justify the opinion, we have laid down.

**) On the 31st of Decbr. 1818 the merchant vessels of the United states measured, officially, 1,225184 $\frac{40}{95}$ Tons.

from Salem *) Boston, New York, Philadelphia, Charleston &c. These bring nankins, teas, muslins, and silks for home consumption, and cotton in great quantities, principally for re - exportation for the supply of the European manufactories. This lucrative carrying - trade, as well as its other branches to Europe, which the government most powerfully supports with its navy, will concentrate itself more and more in the hands of the Americans, whose cedar, Carolina oak, and firs, supply a timber for naval architecture, far superior to that of Europe, in goodness and durability, and who possess on their own soil, every other naval requisite, in the most abundant superfluity. This circumstance, on South America also entering the lists, will be particularly

---

*) Salem containing 15000 inhabitants had about 50 ships round the Cape of Good Hope in 1817, and Boston in 1818 had a similar number; more than 50,000 bales of cotton, containing about 17 millions lbs, and valued at 2 millions of dollars, were exported in the latter year from East India ports in American bottoms, principally, it is true for European consumption; but what prospects open for the future, when this carrying trade, will be changed into one, dedicated to the supply of inland manufactories, and how close at hand, is perhaps this period!?

felt, as it must annihilate a considerable mass of European industry, and the profits arising from it; not taking into consideration, that probably at no very distant period, no European navy, will be able to cope with that of America, provided it be augmented in proportion to the resources and extent of territory in the new continent. In the Northern Union, laws have provided for this gradual increase; and in those states of South America, which are contending for their independence, necessity but more the rapaciousness of dissolute freebooters assembled together from every quarter of the globe, have created a small naval force, which either as defensive or offensive, will during the progress of the war, continually encrease, and, on a solid organization of the different states, taking place, which are at present but formless masses of fermenting matter, is likely to be regularly formed and augmented.

But if the principle be correct, of which England has given us so splendid an example, that, that state will take the lead in commerce, whose navigation is protected and supported by the largest and most expert navy, — Europe will not be able, long to maintain her monopoly to her remaining colonies, against America in a perfect state of freedom, nor continue to wield her trident, when opposed to her rival, who is even dangerous at present, and

(17)

has evidently every advantage on her side. The greater distance, the danger of the European seas, particularly of the Cattegat and the English channel, and the expence of equipment and insurance, more considerable on this account, are so many disadvantages, with which Europe has to contend; whereas, the geographical situation of the European colonies, is eminently favorable to a navigation to and from American ports, and pronounces them, as long as a colonial system is upon the whole to exist, to be much rather natural dependencies of America.

We have already spoken of the West India islands, which will very soon no doubt, follow the impulse, imparted to them by America, in striving at independence, and have hinted at occurrences, which may possibly take place in the East Indies. If we further cast a look to Africa, where such an extensive field for the spirit of discovery and the speculation of trade, lies open; it is evident, that the position of the Western side of this quarter of the globe, is more particularly adapted to an intercourse with the harbours and coasts of the Eastern part of South America, than convenient for the trade hitherto carried on with Europe; it is evident, the coast of Guinea can be frequented with greater facilities, from Caracca, Cayenne and Surinam, and that of Congo, made much quicker from Brazil,

than from any one European port, and that the
Cape of Good Hope, laying directly to the East of
the River Plata, is much better adapted for an intercourse with Rio-Janeiro, Buenos Ayres, and Magellan than for a Dutch or British colony. — Again,
how short is the distance from the Cape, to the Isles
of France, Bourbon, and Madagascar situated between the latter and the Eastern coast of Africa,
and how much more favorably suited, are these possessions for a communication with the new states of
South America, than with their present mother
countries! — And further, how much easier is the
passage to the spice and Philippine islands and
New Holland, being remnants of a former continent, scattered to the South of the coasts of China,
and to the East of the Indian peninsula, from the
Eastern side of America round the Cape, or from
her Western harbours through the Pacific, than from
Great Britain or the Netherlands; and in how much
greater a degree, is this the case with the Marque-
sas, the Friendly and Society islands, in the South
sea, which face the fertile coasts of Lima, of St.
Jago and Valparaiso! An impartial view of the map
of the world is only necessary in fact, to convince
any one, that as soon as the reins of America, are
fallen from the hands of Europe, the intercourse
of the latter with the above possessions, will decline
in proportion, as the means unfold themselves, in

the new continent, of supplying those productions, and manufacturing those goods, requisite for a commercial communication, and of forming those political and moral ties with them, without which, a trading intercourse has no worth! For even the sceptre of intellectual superiority will not be swayed for ever by Europe, should it even be hereditarily inherent in the European race, which however would be difficult to prove; for it is this very race, and by no means its weaker part — which has at all times taken care to remain at home — that has founded and continues to people the regions of the new world, propagating itself not more degenerately most assuredly, than in ancient Europe, and gradually ennobling the different races of the other hemispheres, by a vigorous mixture. The American is inferior to no European nation, and superior to many, in spirit of enterprize, faculty of invention, and corporeal strength and stamina. The arts of war and government have brought forth a Washington, and the sublimer sciences a Franklin; Miranda appeared as it were, a precursory example, of the political and warlike talents which South America was capable of giving birth to, and the present epocha there, is likely yet to develope much, of which posterity will have to judge. The instruction of every branch of useful knowledge, is attended to; the muses are not without their votaries, and the cities of South, rather than of North America, are embellished with monuments of the plastic arts, which may serve to inspire future genius; the missionaries of the Catholic church, engaged in imparting suavity, to the manners of the aboriginal tribes, enrich at the same time the field of science, particularly that of physics, and Humboldt makes mention of respectable names, in all the various paths of human intelligence. Much technical knowledge, considerable talents, and the most persevering energies, will constantly emigrate from Europe, and the freedom of opinion, as well as of every profession, will facilitate the developement of each natural endowment. But, as soon as the intellectual faculties once unshackled, begin to exert themselves on the vast field of both the Americas, and are able to appropriate, the infinite treasures of nature and other resources they possess, to the purposes of dominion, or to the profits of commerce; no other quarter of the world, much less a single people, who have been rendered powerful for a series of time, by the nature of their free civil constitution, but more exalted by the relaxed state of other nations, will be able to dispute the supremacy of the ocean with the new world.

It appears therefore to be less likely, that Europe will be indemnified, for her probable loss of influence, and commercial relation with America, by the extension of her trade, and her transmarine colonial system, than, that in this respect, it may rather be apprehended, America will be continually doing her more and more injury. The question is therefore, if Europe could not, by adopting another line of conduct, in extending her more immediate surrounding frontiers, and following a system more suitable to the new order of things, support the edifice of her wonted greatness, by novel and perhaps more secure foundations? —

X.

As the immediate consequence of the independence of both Americas, and the national progress of their internal culture, and external navigation, we have, in the above reflexions, deduced the failure of the accustomed importations of the precious metals into Europe ; the total want of sale for European productions in the West-Indies and America; and the rise of a powerful competition in the trade, and navigation of the Indian seas. We have hinted at the probable loss of the European colonial establishments

Buenos Aires

The Bridgewater Canal between Worsley and Manchester in England

on the coasts of the other quarters of the world, on
the islands of the grand ocean, and at the consequent stagnation of those branches of industry,
which the commercial preponderance of Europe,
hitherto almost unlimited, has brought to light,
and continually supported; and lastly we have alluded to the encreasing emigration of helpless multitudes, from their paternal soil. To prevent Europe
from falling to decay, countries at present flourishing, from being again changed into deserts, the
habitations of ingenious application and active industry from being deserted, harbours choaked up, and
the sublimer cultivation of the mind, (which in general is only to be found, where man is independent
of physical wants) from being totally neglected,
an equivalent must at least be found in the course
of time, for the above losses, and life returning
into the exhausted veins, must be made to flow into
new channels. No other possibility of accomplishing this, presents itself, than that, of Europe instead of operating as hitherto, principally abroad,
directing her attention for the future, to herself,
and endeavoring to replace by internal trade, what
she may have lost in foreign intercourse. This conduct she ought to pursue, until, by no very impro-
bable concatenation of future events, an opportunity
offer itself even to her, of re-acquiring, no monopoly — for that seems to be lost for ever — but a

share of the grand commerce of the world, suitable to the situation she fills and compatible with her natural wealth. We will explain ourselves clearer on this subject. —

The discovery of the new continent, and that made by Vasco de Gama, of the passage to the East Indies, round the Cape of Good Hope, have checked the internal exploration of Europe and the culture of her own natural resources; have stamped the minds of men, with a longing after foreign enjoyments, and have given industry a tendency, to the production of articles, of more consequence for the the luxury of the rich, and calculated better for a trade to transatlantic acquisitions, than corresponding with the real wants of the mass of the people, and the general welfare, which is always more promoted, by the most animated adjoining intercourse, than by distant commercial enterprizes on a large scale.

No state has more bitterly felt the disadvantages, of a system of aggrandizement, founded on transmarine possessions, than the one, who gave birth to this spirit; we mean the Spanish peninsula, including Portugal, which is almost indivisible from it, in every natural, political and oeconomical point of view. What near sources of prosperity are here dried up! The precious metals lay useless in the bosom of the mountains; instead of possessing

superfluous means of nourishment, which a fruitful
soil, in unison with the finest climate, are capable
of producing; this favored country is almost continually in want of foreign grain; its cities and
villages have become more and more desolate *), its

---

*) The population of Spain, as is generally known,
amounts hardly now to 11 millions; it contained
under the most flourishing period of the Arabian
dominion, double this number, not to speak of
the times of the Roman sovereignty. The following information, taken from the Börsen - Halle
newspaper of 1819 (No. 2146) affords the most
striking proof, of the low state, to which the
internal oeconomical welfare of this kingdom is
sunken:

> ''Madrid the 16th June.
''The importation of grain from the Crim,
''the Levant and even the North American
''states, continues into those provinces which
''are situated on the sea, whilst the corn in
''the provinces of the interior, has no value
''whatever. It comes cheaper to import it
''from Odessa into Barcellona, and from Phi-
''ladelphia into Corunna, than to transport it
''from the interior''.

This almost incredible account will be intelligible, on calling to mind the description, which

(18)

forests are without culture and neglected; and
Northern and even American mariners have engrossed its navigation in the Mediterranean, at the entrance of which, nature seems to have placed it as
a guardian. And does the British empire, indebted for its greatness, to the commerce of the world,
founded upon the colonial system, present internally a picture of harmony, on which the eye of the
philanthropist could rest with the most perfect
satisfaction, and acknowledge it, with a just sense
of feeling, to be the summit of all earthly exertions?
The sunken state of Ireland, this island so richly
favored by nature, darkens the view, and the magnificence and splendour of the palaces of European
Nabobs, containing every thing, worthy of the production of man, and what the most refined arts of

---

Bourgoing, (Tableau de l'Espagne moderne: II.
p. 161.) makes of the difficulties of internal communication: Quelques unes de ces provinces, re-
cueillent assés souvent plus de grains qu'elles ne
peuvent en consommer. Mais les difficultés pour
la circulation interieure rendent cette fertilité
à peu près inutile au reste du royaume. Peu
de chemins, pas une riviére navigable,
pas un canal, qui soit en pleine acti-
vité: Aussi les moyens de transports sont-ils
très lents et très dispendieux. —

enjoyment, have been capable of assembling for the
delight of the children of fortune, can on no account
parget the crying misery of the contantly encreasing
multitude of poor, as little as the solid wealth and
prosperity of the most respectable middle-classes,
are able to do away with the picture of distressing
indigence, felt by so many thousands of labourers,
on whose ill-rewarded industry, the over-rich master founds his proud independence. The height of
human happiness, does most undoubtedly, not bloss-
om there, where such rough contrasts, connected
which each other, by no softer shades, are to be
found. We are not alluding to the moral state of
this country, our view being entirely directed to its
political situation; but we venture to utter this
conviction, that the irresistible impending change
of relation, in which Great Britain stands at present
to the rest of the world, may most undoubtedly be
injurious to her power of dominion, but is likely
rather to be advantageous to her internal prosperity.
But this will only be the case, provided the future
policy of Europe considered as a body, allow each of
her members, to prosecute their several aims, as
long as they come under an universal system of
legality, without injury to the rights of others, upon
a basis of unshackled competition, and freed from
the provocations and chichanes of jealousy and
egoism. —

For there is alone salvation for Europe, under the stipulation, that, as America is powerful by the plenitude of her liberties, yet combined under one common tie, Europe also henceforth consider herself as forming one grand state, which, although not actually united under one central power, but governing herself upon the principles of one common interest, and one public spirit, as far as regards her relation to other parts of the world, be ever ready to uphold the natural fundamental laws of every organized union, by opposing the strength of all to the aggressions of a few. Looked upon in this light, the ancient queen of the world is still powerful and glorious, without her transmarine empire, and is deficient, according to no degenerate estimation, in no one desirable production of nature, and none of the elements necessary to raise man to the most dignified state of perfection. From the Ural mountains to the Atlantic ocean, which washes the western coasts of the Hebrides down to the chain of the Algarvian hills, and from the northernmost part of Lapland to the furthermost point of Sicily, or the heel of ancient Peleponnesus, so celebrated in history; what an assemblage of costly territories, what richness in forests, lakes, and rivers, what fruitful vallies, and cultivated plains, what fulnes in wine and oil, what blessings in herds and flocks, what hidden treasures of

precious stones, what abundance of salubrions wa-
ters, and what climates, mild and austere, present
themselves, admirably suited, to cherish and preserve the pure ancient race, transplanted hither in
the remotest ages, to invigorate the mind, and without effeminating them, to refresh the senses , with
all the joys and abundance of life! Where else,
flourish so fine a race of men, where does feminine
exquisiteness, free yet reserved and domestic, charm-
ing yet full of modesty, lovely still at the same
time dignified, develope itself as in Europe; where
is woman to be found, as here, possessing equal
rights in the monogamous mariage state, ennobled
by education, and by the habits of the stronger sex
even more powerful, than the apparent ruler, who
offers up his strength at the shrine of loveliness?
And further, the ancient civilization, a work accomplished thousands of years ago, by cultivated nations
who inhabited this portion of the globe, the treasures of language, of arts and science, — what advantages are these, if Europe understood to retain them!
— Do not let us assert, that Europe is become antiquated; nature continues eternally young, and re-
novates itself from its own means; but her power is dissipated abroad in a space, which she is incapable of filling, and those resources she yet possesses for operating upon her internal properity,
are inimically turned against herself, not alone by

the bloody wars of one state against another, but
almost more so, by the eternal conflict of self-ambi-
tion, envious rivalship in trade, and a jealous view
of the grandeur and improvement of the neighbour!
If things are to remain thus, the exhaustion of
every source of foreign supplies, must be injurious
to us, and our own welfare will never prosper. For
Europe will never enjoy her own natural blessings,
until her rulers abjuring all little considerations,
are happily bold enough, to compass the above grand
idea of One European state body. This must take
place 'ere those fatal partitions can be removed,
which at present sever state from state, or in reality, one member of the same body from the other,
and which are the means of keeping them upon a
hostile footing, in like manner as the savage is
continually armed and prepared for defence or for
attacking his neighbour. And is not Europe, then,
physically considered, one single organized body?
Do not her rivers and her mountains extend their
course in common through her territories? and are
all these not washed by the same ocean, which
appears to have forced its way, through narrow
channels to the North and the South, in order to
reach them all, and render them jointly partakers
of its benefits? And are not the productions of her
soil unequally distributed under her different regions
in order that no one part, shall be able to dispense

with the other, and that no one country have it in its power to exclude any member of the same community? —

But under the influence of our perverseness, and political jealousy, scorning the dictates of nature, we have acted upon a different plan; we have invented prohibitions of importation and exportation directed against our reighbours, we have imagined the blockade of harbours and closing of rivers; we have devised privileges, and monopolizing trading companies; and we have contrived manufacturing and commercial systems, in order absurdly to produce and supply that, which can be obtained cheaper from our neigbours, whilst the natural productions of our own soil, which could be prepared and manufactured for the use of the latter, remain often neglected, or are undersold in a raw state, for an inconsiderable price. And to us belong the fruits of such unnatural endeavours; we reap the misery of wars carried on for the purposes of commerce, and of those engaged in, for the gratification of private ambitious aims, we labour under the nuisance and evil effects, of illegal trade and defraudation of the revenue, which make the coasts and frontiers of the different countries, (which ought, as under the American Union to stand cordially inviting, open to each

neigbour *) rendezvous of a morally depraved rabble,
who transgressing unnatural laws, occupy an inqui-
sitorial branch of justice, which, but too often, wink-
ing at thinly disguised artifices, dishonors its name
by guilty connivances, and introducing a degree of remissness into this most partial system, renders the selfish views of the government abortive !

---

*) "No taxes or impositions shall be levied on goods
"which are exported from one state to another.
"By any regulations of trade or of duties, the
"ports of one state shall not enjoy a preference
"to those of any other, nor shall ships, going to
"or from one state, be bound to touch at another,
"or be subject to any duty. — No state, without
"the permission of Congress, shall levy imports
"and exports, except so many, as are necessary
"to put its laws of inspection into force. The
"net produce of all imposts and duties, which
"are laid by one State on exports and imports,
"flows into the treasury of the Uuited states,
"and all such laws are subject to the inspection
"and controul of Congress. No state shall levy
tonnage-dues without permission of Congress."
— Constitution of the government of the Union
&c 1st Article.

If all these things are to remain, as they are at present *), a vigorous renovation of our quarter of the globe is not to be imagined, and Europe will go p i e c e - m e a l to ruin, in proportion, as America by unanimity, and a legally free developement of her resources, will consolidate her dominion. Nevertheless, the present prospects argue more the hope of a better fate, than the dread of a contrary one. Europe has experienced the consequences of her internal weakness and her external discord, by the ignominious oppression, which she endured from the late daring subjugator, who unconditionally commanding the whole resources of One single kingdom, with this power attacked the rest in their isolation, and seized upon one after the other. Europe has passed through all the deformities of phantastic constitutions, and seems to persist in a representative form of government. But it appears peculiar to this constitution, to direct its attention to the internal welfare, and the secret defects of the

---

*) From a petition, that has been lately laid before parliament and signed by the p r i n c i p a l merchants in London, it is to be hoped, that the restrictive system of trade hitherto pursued by England, will be subject to modifications.

(19)

state, and at the same time, to oppose a salutary
counterpoise to the natural tendency of the government which is directed towards abroad. It may reasonably be expected, as far as regards the former of
these objects, that the obstacles which stand most
in the way of the internal welfare of the generality
of states, will above all, first be the subjects of consideration. These we consider to be; the legal inequalities of privileged and oppressed religious per-
suasions, the disproportionate principles of taxation,
and the personal and local exemptions from bearing
the common burthens, the inequality of the standard, and every defect of the pecuniary currency,
the difference of the weights and measures, the deficiency of internal communications, the prohibi-
tory game laws on the one side, and the uncontrouled exercise of the chace on the other, every species
of villainage, consisting either in personal or real
acts of servitude, or in labour which is wholly un-
requited, the accise and customs, as far as these are
prejudicial to the productions and trade of a country,
and the restrictive systems of guilds and corpora-
tions, as far as they shackle the industry of the arti-
ficer and manufacturer. But the more progress,
that individual states make in an enquiry into these
evils, and the means of remedying them, and the
more publicity which be given to individual successful results, the more, men will be aware, that the

system of isolation and hostility hitherto pursued, must by an injurious external counter-operation, paralize every good which may have been effected internally, and thus, reciprocal approaches towards the universal benefit of a European state-union, will be facilitated. —

But it is not alone the new and better principles (the fruit of most bitter trials, and painful purifications) by which the several governments appear at present to be actuated, that entitle us to the hope, that an understanding as alluded to above, and most devoutly to be wished for, will not be once more stifled in its birth, by the ancient machinations of politics; but it is also the counterpoise of a novel free popular spirit, which has burst forth every where, be it in new constitutions, or even in the maxims and acts of political bodies, and which presents a barrier to tyranny, and the thirst after aggrandizement. Neither is it likely, that the necessary instrument of this latter passion, a standing army, forming as hitherto a state in the state, will stand much longer at its command, in the extended sense it has done since the time of Louis the fourteenth *). The ancient system followed in Prussia,

---

*) We only quote here the example of Great Britain whose standing army ever proportionably

and copied by most other governments, of recruit-
ing the standing army by means of soldiers of
every nation, will cease, as being inadequate to protect, and far inferior to the actual resources of a
country; partly because, the free man, who cannot
find support at home, will rather seek it on a foreign
soil, than enlist himself under foreign colours for
bad pay, and partly on account of the low state of
the public finances every where, being unable to
support such armies of ostentation. But the more the
public encouragement of the common - weal encreases, and the more peremptorily, the failure of foreign supplies, must summon even the weakest
understanding, to repair the loss from the native
soil, the smaller the number will be, of the internal population in every state, which will be levied
for permanent service. For the truth, |now most
generally acknowledged, will at length be fully
established, that every citizen is a member of the
national army, and as snch, must be exercised and
qualified for defending his hearth and country; but
that the permanent army ought only to consist of

---

the smallest, was considerably augmented during
the late truly national war, but immediately on
peace taking place, was reduced, and will be
still further diminished, there is scarcely any
doubt.

the leaders and those necessary for exercising the troops, and in short only of what is artificially expressed by the c a d r e s of an army, which those classes capable of bearing arms and already exercised, should be obliged to join, fully equipped on the first summons of any danger. With armies like these America fought her emancipation, and with such, every state at all times, will be best enabled to defend its liberties; no man but a Napoleon could misuse armed national masses for the subjugation of Europe; but a thousand years only bring forth one such character, and the age in which he lived, alone favored his advancement; but it was not the skilful armies of the potentates, but the spirit that animated the whole mass of their subjects, which levelled him with the dust. —

If the twofold problem of our age were thus solved, in allowing the nations, in understanding with their governments, to consult thenselves, upon their own welfare, which stimulus they even received from the congress of Vienna *), and at the same time in rendering them capable of defending them-

---

*) See the "last act of the Vienna congress of the 9th June 1816" — (according to Klüber's second edition, Erlangen 1818) § 1. and the German act of Confederation § 13.

selves, by accustoming them to the use of arms, without, on that account withdrawing the flower of their men, by continual military duty, from productive industy, on which the welfare of the state depends; the finances would no longer have occasion, to squander away their best and readiest revenues, upon the maintenance of standing armies; the people wonld experience considerable alleviation, and many taxes, at variance with the higher purposes of state-oeconomy, would fall away. Then, but not before, the earth would be duly employed in every species of production, be it in mining, agriculture, or the growth and care of its forests, and those dispositions for the promotion of internal and external communication, would be quickly and energetically made, of which, in many parts of Europe, the outlines only exist, and which are no where arrived at perfection, except perhaps in England. By these resources, which are the means of shortening distances, and bringing man and man nearer together, the surplus produce of one territory could be conveniently transported for the benefit of the other; and it would be impossible for the future, for one member of the whole body, then more intimately connected, to be languishing in want whilst another state from false motives of fear, or envious speculation shuts up its frontiers, in order to withhold the expected supplies of aid, in the critical moment of distress. On the solid foundation of such an improved use being made of the soil, a new manufacturing system would arise of itself, which not occupied in producing large masses of goods for distant quarters of the world, would direct its atten-tion principally to the supply of internal necessi-ties; we should be decked out less with the luxuries of both the Indies, but the improved majority of the people, would be more substantially fed and better clothed, and those enjoyments, of which Europe possesses such superfluity, would be more generally accessible to it. A far more extensive degree of prosperity would every where take place, unalloyed by an overbearing load of wealth, and a nobler sense of attachment to the paternal soil, rendered more consolatary to inhabit, would be felt by all ranks. On the states becoming more friendly inclined to each other, the mass of population, would volunta-rily distribute itself more equally over the face of Europe; for oppression alone, and a partial surplus of inhabitants in some parts, together with prohibi-tory laws, local constraints, and the want of inter-nal communications, but on no account an absolute superfluity of population in the whole of Europe, has caused the late emi-grations to transatlantic territories. The centre of Europe is at present the best employed, and most numerously peopled; strong colonies of agricultural and manufacturing hands could still find room and useful occupation, on her Western extremity, and in extensive tracts towards her Eastern and Southern frontiers; and it is entirely the fault of the European nations in common, in losing their children, by emigration to foreign climes, and wasting their blood and most vigorous strength, in subjugating the Mahratta states to a commercial company, keeping the king of Candy in obedience, or in ruling the straits of Magellan and Mallacca, whilst they are not even masters on their own territory. For does not the kingdom of the Osmans, from the limits of Hungary and Transylvania to the shores of Asia Minor, form a part of European soil? Have not its cities and villages, its monuments of ancient art and science, been built and founded by the most chosen of the European nations, and only become the prey of an Asiatic barbarian people', through the contentions of the Christian world? And do not the descendants of the Helenists, groaning under the tyranny of the above conquerors, in vain sigh for liberation? And have the above people, now in possession for near four hundred years, of such an extensive territory under the most lovely climate, endeavored to approach or assimulate themselves to the European, to introduce amongst them, the free sentiments, the noble institutions, the arts and science of the latter? And do

they not even remain to the present day, in blind
Oriental supineness, unsociable, and not allied by
any ties of blood, directly opposed to European culture, formidable by their very indolence, which
freely admits the entrance of the most horrible of
evils, under which mankind, incapable of defence,
sinks, and which can only be kept at a distance,
but not subdued?

, This alone wonld be a sufficient justification
for the Christian European nations, putting an end
to this Turkish nuisance; for the welfare of states
and the lives of their citizens, ought not to be exposed, without protection and defence, to those calamities, which nature in her chaotic eruptions, may
overhwelm them with; for the destination of man
on earth, just consists in rendering nature subject
to him, and in improving and perfecting it, according to the dictates of reason. For this very cause,
no lasting peace, but only an armistice, is imaginable with a people who do not acknowledge the
above destiny of man, but passing their existence,
under a despotic government in a state of anarchy
and lawlessness, are subject to the arbitrariness of
their ruler, and to a blind fatality, founded on a
system of predestinate superstition, which proves an
insurmountable barrier to every active advance of
rational improvement. Europe can never lay down

(20)

her arms, as long as her South-eastern territories are in possession of a people, incapable of raising themselves to the idea of a legally political union, and who are liable to watch only the moment of tranquillity, for invading the heart of our quarter of the globe, with the same desperate fury, which hurried them across the Hellespont.

If, as has been asserted, and which many preparatory events seem to confirm, Catharine of Russia, entertained the daring scheme, of extending her kingdom from the Black sea to the Archipelagus, and raising Constantinople once more to the seat of a Christian empire, this plan might not appear sufficiently ripe for the age she lived in, and might seem impracticable, from the then existing unsteady and jealous politics of the European powers, who would hardly have permitted such an aggrandizement; but it was nevertheless a grand idea, and beneficial to the general welfare of Europe, and it may yet one day be carried into execution, the more the common interests of this whole portion of the globe, become the subject of consideration. But to her belongs the glory, of having begun this great work, and of having formed settlements on the Northern coast of the Black sea, the ancient seat of Grecian refinement, of which Odessa at least, has already risen to a high state of prosperity, and has been admitted as a reciprocal operative member

in the system of European commerce *). But this
plan cannot be fully developed, or completed in
itself, before the Dardanelles, under European protection and dominion, become accessible to all nations. For this purpose, in concert with the whole
of Europe, Russia could lend a helping hand from
the Dniester and Austria from the Danube, and
the reconquest of the present Turkish !provinces,
with the cooperation in the North, of the Servians
attached to freedom, and the New-Grecian races in
the South, would not probably be so difficult a task,
as the expulsion of the Moors formerly from Spain.
If then, as lays in the nature of the idea, having
formerly existed in reality, a Christian empire were
founded in Constantinople, in the ¡centre of the
Adriatic gulph, and the Black sea; and from the

---

*) "In the year 1794 there was not a living soul
"nor a hut on the spot where Odessa now stands.
"At present (1818) this city has already ¡1000
"stone houses and above 40,000 inhabitants.
"Above 800 ships leave her harbour annually,
"and there is so much corn exported from thence,
"that this neighbourhod, will shortly become,
"what is was in the Grecian and Roman æras,
"a granary for supplying the countries in the
"Mediterrranean". — Political Journal for 1818.
1st Vol. P. 199.

South point of Morea upwards, as far as where the Sawe empties itself into the Danube, and along the banks of this river, until it loses itself in the Euxine, a point of "appui" were found, capable, of supporting and organizing every further plan, towards reestablishing Europe's pristine glory, and consolidating her communication with Asia and Africa.

The reunion of the islands of the Archipelagus with the newly formed empire, would necessarily follow of itself; and, as in ancient times, colonies would flourish on the Southern shores of the seas bounding Europe, on the Pontus, in Asia Minor, and in Northern Africa, which at present is subservient to the Turks. For Europe is never secure from the attacks of barbarians, and fresh popular inundations, until she again become mistress of her entire natural territory, aud her opposite shores, be reinstated in civilization, European manners, and a friendly commercial intercourse. Cæsarea and Carthage, Cyrene and Alexandria, must arise again; under the Ægis of Europe, Miletus, Ephesus and Smyrna, must become enlightened and free; and from Propontis to the promontory of Rhetium, a chain of industrious cities must be formed, such as the ancient world boasted of, principally in Prusa, and Nicomedia, Chalcedon, Sinope and Trapezus.

Such is the true colonial system of Europe, to accomplish, and establish which, we trust considerable

armies' will be made use of, for the last time! —
Here is employment for a century; here prospects
open of a cheering state of prosperity, and a ready
commercial intercourse, which contributes to the
happiness of both people and countries; and the
productions of Eastern India, would once more flow
through the Arabian gulph, into Alexandria, again
the seat of animation. The Crusades, under other
pretences but with a just impulse, and the later
Turkish wars, had precisely these objects in view.
The discovery of America, has thrown Europe out of
her natural course; it will require time for her to
resume the forsaken track, lighted by the torch of
history, and conspicuously pointed out, by the sublimest monuments of art.

XI.

We hope that intelligent readers, well versed in
history, not unacquainted with the revolution of
events, and who are enabled to view futurity from
the past, will not reject the above picture of a
future state of Europe, as the offspring of a romantic, and extravagant imagination; but will

rather recognize therein, outlines, which the spirit
of the times is unceasingly striving to model into
lasting forms and to realize which, necessity irresist-
ibly inclines, but must be cordially supported in
the task, by a ready willingness. In the mean time,
we do not pretend to deny, that a period of time,
of indefinite length, lays between the present and
the above future æra, which can on no account be
s p r u n g o v e r, but must be w a d e d t h r o u g h;
and that this interval, on the brink of which, the
present generation seems to stand, will not be the
most cheering. On this, we return to the actual
road of observation, and shall endeavour to develope
and illustrate, in their probable connexion, the
nearest consequences of the grand event of the complete emancipation of America.

We shall confine ourselves in the first place to
that occurrence, which must above all, undoubtedly
take place, and in its endless ramifications, must
penetrate and change the whole texture of the political relation and social intercourse of the civilized world, — we mean the failure of hose supplies
of the precious metals hitherto enjoyed by Europe.
From what has been said before, this may be considered as unavoidable, on tribute no longer flowing
into the treasuries of Enropean sovereigns, or of
those Grandees holding possessions in America, and
on payment ceasing for those European articles,

which America once her own misstress, will produce herself; that a continually encreasing scarcity of ready money in Europe,
must be the consequences of these events, cannot
but be evident. But other causes will unite with
the above, in rendering the precious metals more
rare, which will also multiply the general distress,
and enhance the difficulty of keeping the existing
means of currency in circulation. We allude to
the stagnation of so many branches of industry, hitherto in activity for the West Indies and America,
which had been employed either directly in the production of the necessaries and articles of luxury,
requisite for the wants of the above countries, or
indirectly, in keeping up the extensive European
navigation, which must decline yearly, in proportion as that of America will encrease; and circumstances like these, will also encourage the propensity of amassing or treasuring the precious metals.
For every stagnation in productive industry or
commercial influence, necessarily renders the circulation of money from hand to hand more inert;
the duller it is, consequently the greater difficulties there arise for those who are in want, in obtaining money, the more every individual, partly from
the necessity of not becoming embarrassed, and
partly from excessive caution, will feel inclined,
to deposit in his own keeping, a larger quantity

of his ready cash, than he otherwise would do, if he had the prospect of turning his capital quickly over, by employing it in some lucrative undertakiug, at a period of an animated commercial traffic. For this reason, thinly peopled countries, having but little internal trade, stand in need of more cash in proportion, than those, wherein the circulation is brisk, and is renewed several times annually; it is therefore why, a greater accumulation of precious metals out of circulation, is to be met with in averaged poor states, such as Poland and different Russian provinces, than in those, where industry and trade vibrate with animated motion. But the joint operation of all these circumstances, appears to forebode a total revolution in the pecuniary system of all Europe. We shall in the first place view it, as far as it relates to the finances, and the public debts of the several states.

Here we offer the remark, that, almost every country without exception, is at present in a state of embarrassment, less occasioned by the difficulty of providing for its actual wants, than by that, of repaying capitals long since squandered away, which have been anticipated from the public income. This circumstance is principally derived from the propensity for aggrandizement, (so often mentioned) congenial to states, and the inclination inherent in them, as in individuals, of exceeding the bounds of their natural income. The usual revenue of the states, consisting of the permanent taxes paid by the people, was impossible to satisfy this propensity, and the wars which were the fruit of it; neither were extraordinary imposts, which were laid on the subjects in the customary manner, adequate to accomplish the purposes of despotism and ambition. The trial was then made, to turn the contribution to the real or imaginary necessities of the state, which could no longer be supported by the ordinary means of revenue, into a lucrative speculation, by loans on advantageous conditions, whereby the governments got into their power, for a longer or shorter space of time, those disposeable capitals which were possessed at home, or were to be procured from abroad. In doing this, they were rolling the burthens of the time present, upon posterity, without considering, how the latter would be able to find the means of bearing the weight of its own engagements, besides that of past generations, and of providing repayment for capitals, long since spent and dissipated on useless undertakings. It is so evident, that such a system in the administration of a state, as well as in the domestic oeconomy of every private individual, must lead to ruin, if carried on longer, than there are means of bearing the encreasing burthen, that it would be inconceivable, why this view of the case did not lead to

154

more moderation, if the experience of all ages did
not sufficiently teach us, that the pressure and the
passions of the present moment, almost invariably
overcome every consideration for the future. But
still the mischief might have had bounds prescribed
it, and a hope of bringing back things to their former state, might have been indulged, had not the
general confusion reached its highest pitch, by the
unfortunate idea of raising to a financial resource,
a pure mercantile expedient: the issuing of a draft
on funds, actually existing and in deposit, instead
of repeatedly paying the same out; whereby assign-
ments on monies, no where extant, were issued,
and representatives, of no intrensic value were clothed with the public authority of legal tenders for
payment *) For as long as the affairs of a state are
conducted by means of hard cash, the possibility of
encreasing its expences, is limited to the possibility
of being supplied with this money, which is never
to be obtained without an equivalent of the same
value, consequently depends wholly on the product-

*) The author has published his ideas on the cre-
dit of a country and on paper currency, in a
work, intitled; "On the nature of money and
"the pecuniary currency in a state": Copenhagen 1813.

ive resources of the country; but the system of paper-money, requires in its commencement no such considerations, and an ample space of time elapses, ere the evil becomes so sensible, as to be limited by its own excess. To what lengths this mischief can be carried, and how long it can be forcibly maintained, by the power of the government, amougst others, the history of the French assignats, and the fate of the paper-money issued to redeem them, sufficiently shew. Nevertheless, the most states are under the constant influence of this system, and by the emission of a paper-money, promising future payment of the sum it represents, have, besides their load of debt bearing interest, burthened themselves with a new one of another species. Such is not liable to interest it is true, but in its consequences, by the fluctuating value, and final depreciation, which seem to be the inevitable fate of the best paper-currency, it injures and preys upon the internal welfare of the state, and on private pecuniary exchanges, more sensibly, than public loans contracted in the usual manner are ever capable of doing.

The picture of the public debt of Europe must create astonishment, and it is a most inauspicious phenomenon, that five sevenths of the public income of the British empire are employed in paying the interest on anticipations, which have been made on future resources; for a

debt in its extreme analysis, is nothing more, than
the pre-appropriation of funds not yet existing; or
in other words, that instead of discharging the necessities of the present, these five sevenths are used in
meeting the engagements of times long past.
Through this state of things, it has, by degrees come
to this point, that by far the greater part of the
contributors, must extort the amount of their taxes
from the soil, or from other branches of industry,
in order only to pay them to an (at least in this
respect) idle consumer, in the form of a government annuity, who, had such an institution never
existed, instead of lending his capital to the state,
in whose hands it has remained unproductive, or is
usually squandered away, would have employed it
in some useful undertaking, from which he might
have derived his subsistence; whereas he is now
involuntarily obliged to remain in the class of mere
consumers, being unable to withdraw his capital at
pleasure. It is of no use objecting to this, that
every holder of government paper or stock, is at
liberty to turn it into disposeable capital, by sale at the
stock-market, at the existing price, like any other
exchangeable article. Upon the whole this alters
nothing in the proportion, in which, the class of those
deriving an idle and unproductive income from the
interest of the public funds, stands to the industrious
and productive orders of the state; such a transfer

of stock only changing the former annuitant into an active member of society, and associating the purchaser, who had formerly laboured to the advantage of the state, with the class of annuitants. But supposing the purchase of stock were made for account of a sinking fund, destined for the gradual liquidation of the public debt; the repayment of a capital, taken by these means out of advantageous circulation, would only v i r t u a l l y be restored to it, on no similar amount, on the other hand, being withdrawn from it, at the same time, by the contracting of new debts. But as long as this is usually the case, which daily experience teaches us, the proportion of the above classes remains unchanged, or alters even for the worse. — By these means, it is true, the rich and monied classes of the people, become bound by the closest ties to the state, and to its continuance under its existing forms; but the links of the chain may be twisted so tort, that a single crack will be sufficient violently to burst the whole. For in a state where the greatest part of the revenue is absorbed by the public debt, the income of the country will not suffer a diminution by any event whatsoever, be it some general calamity, a partial decrease of the taxes, or a voluntary retrenchment in the expences. The existing mechanism of states being already limited, by the swelling encrease of the public debt, to the very verge of the expences, necessary for its support, can afford to sacrifice nothing considerable; and the interest of the public debt must be paid, otherwise not alone every idea of credit will vanish, bnt that portion of the nation possessed of the greatest intelligence, and of most influence, who derives its income from this debt, will lose its weight, and the present order of things, with the social union of the different classes of people composing a state, are liable to be subverted from their very foundations. The decided preponderance in trade, and the command of those masses ef gold and silver, hitherto at the power of Europe, have alone enabled Great Britain punctually to fulfill her engagements, whilst France has sunk several times beneath the load of her's, and not alone to find the annual resources for a public deht of near 900 millions of pounds sterling, but by the infinite credit of her government, to retain the means of almost yearly encreasing this debt. With the decay of her influence in commerce, and the decrease of the circulation of bullion in Europe, the possibility of her performing such enormous engagements must naturally cease, and the edifice of her national greatness towering at present to the skies, must be precipitated upon its sinking foundations. The suspension of the Bank of England, from paying its notes in specie, continued so long, and the almost fearful circumspection, with which the exactions of

a future resumption of this measure, have been ac-
compagnied, may serve as warning prognostics.
But should even this promised payment in specie,
actually take place *), the bank of England alone,
and the paper it has in circulation, are covered by
this measure, as long as it may be adhered to; its
adoption has no influence in itself, upon the possibility of liquidating the national debt in the long-
run, which is indeed paid, by order of government,
by the bank, but not from its means: for the soli-
dity of this debt depends entirely on the amount of
the revenue and the resources of the government,
who again rely on the capacity of the people in bearing the present burthens undiminished, for the
future, but these again repose upon the unimpaired
receipts of the country, that is to say, on the continued command of the commerce of the world. But
as the foregoing discussion of this subject, offers reasons, completely at variance, with the undiminished duration of such a commercial preponderance, a
total overthrow of the present system of finance is
not alone to be apprehended in Great Britain, but

---

*) Since the publication of the first edition of this
work, this has been carried into effect, at the
period, and under the restrictions, stipulated by
parliament,

in as far as she constitutes the pulse of the whole pecuniary life of Europe, in the continental states also; and it remains for us to enquire, what turn things are likely to take, political oeconomy resting entirely at present, on the existing relative value of money. —

When the precious metals as m e r c h a n d i z e, become scarcer in a limited sphere of circulation; they will also as c o i n assume a higher price; the eagerness for their possession and use, will render their owners more disinclined to part with them, and will determine him, who stands in need of them, to give, above their usual exchangeable value, an equivalent adequate to the difficulty of obtaining them; in other words, the same quantity of metal of a certain fineness, or a coin of equal weight and standard, will under the above circumstances, pay for a larger quantity of merchandize, than could have been bought for it, before the precious metals became more rare. We shall in this respect once more approach the times, when the same measure of corn, which is now paid with two ounces of silver, cost before the discovery of America, half an ounce only. But the further we advance towards this approximation, the less it will be possible, for the state to demand or obtain the same quantity of precious metal in taxes, which it was enabled to levy, prior to this catastrophe. For that subject for example, who was taxed at 2 ounces of silver, when this sum was equal to one measure of corn, cannot, without being taxed higher, that is, unjustifiably curtailed in his income, p y more than half an ounce of silver or the fourth part of the former amount of his taxes, in the same coin, if this half ounce of silver, is really capable of supplying the state with the intended value of one measure of corn. If he his obliged nothwithstanding, to pay higher taxes, for example one ounce of silver, he only pays, it is true, nominally the half, but virtually the double of his former assessment. But as it will be impossible to inforce this, for any duration of time, it may be taken for granted, that the numerical quantity of the income of the government will decrease, as the value of the precious metals rise in proportion, to those articles, from the exchange of which, the subject must pay his taxes. If therefore a state had retained, with the exception of the decrease of the precious metals, every other source of emolument and prosperity, instead of a former income of 40 millions of dollars, it would only be able to calculate upon one of 10 millions for the future, in the same coin. But on this it follows immediately, that the state calculating its expences upon the same scale, cannot likewise pay its creditor, more than a fourth part of the nominal amount in the same coin,

(22)

as interest; and that as soon as things in general have found their level, he ought to be perfectly satisfied with this reduction, for in reality he will be able to provide for the same wants, procure the same enjoyments, and pay for the same services and labor with his nominally reduced income, as he could have done before. In this manner then, justice would in fact be duly administered, but the government, which reduced a capital, or its contracted engagements in the proportion of 4 to 1, had ostensibly made a bankruptcy, which, considering the intermediate state, that must be past through, before a rule generally just, could be conveniently accommodated to all particular cases and exigences, would be attended most undoubtedly with individual inconformities and disadvantages, but which must sooner or later be considered nevertheless as inevitable. It ought to be the first consideration of a state, convinced of the necessity of this nominal bankruptcy, to organize it so, as to be as harmless as possible.

To effect this, only two expedients appear to present themselves; namely, that of keeping up the nominal amount of all engagements made in money which could then be discharged by a currency depreciated according to circumstances, and agreable to the example we have chosen above, by coin containing but one quarter of the gold or silver, the

ancient ones of the same name did; or that, of reducing the nominal amount of all stipulated pay-
ments, according to the augmented value, which
money may have assumed in regard to merchandize
and the price of labour, — by which a demand of
100 dollars, could legally be liquidated by 25 dollars
in the ancient undebased coin *).

The principles of these two systems are so syno-
nymous, that it is perfectly indifferent, which of
them the government might think proper to follow;
but above all things it ought to be carefully avoid-
ed, not to allow such a measure to anticipate the proper period, or to be put into force as an arbitrary
initiative, founded on the self interest of the government. The precise time onght to be so chosen the-

---

*) In states, which had to free themselves from a
   depreciated paper currency, and to regulate stipulated engagements, made at different periods,
   besides similar measures having been adopted, a
   reduction of the paper money was also made
   upon the principle of time; by virtue of which,
   the same nominal debt according to the value,
   which it bore in hard silver, at the time it was
   contracted, can be liquidated by very different
   sums, in the new standard money. It is evident
   that a double reduction occurs in cases of this
   nature.

refore, that it would not be necessary to a n n o u n c e
a change, but o n l y to s a n c t i o n that which
had already taken place, and simply to p u b l i s h
the rise in value of the precious metals, now become
scarcer, which had long before been felt in the general operations of commerce, and in the intercourse
of daily exchange, and agreable to it, to regulate
with moderation and equity, the relation of the different classes of society, interwoven with each other
by pecuniary transactions. Of the two alternatives
which have been proposed, the former appears more
suited to the nature of the case and the convenience
of civil life, than the latter. For as necessity and
custom have introduced since time immemorial,
the exchange of merchandize according to certain
quantities and measures, which being grown together, as it were, with the roots of civilized institutions, must be looked upon as lasting and permanent; it is nothing more than just, that the metals,
as precious wares given in exchange for it, should
be coined upon such a scale, as according to their
intrinsic value, might easiest offer an equivalent
to the above weights and measures. The people
would be less perplexed and embarrassed in their
calculations, if their dealings carried on in ducats,
crowns and groats or marks, skillings and pfennings,
were continued for the future agreable to this scale
in a lighter money, than if, for the sake of the

ancient heavy coin, which could perhaps pay for three
or four times the usual quantity of merchandize,
they should be obliged to calculate according to perfectly strange fractions, in unfamiliar quantities and
their respective subdivisions. To this may be added;
that in the present state of society — where the
immediate exchange of material necessities, is completely supplanted by the intervention of money;
and labour, contrary to the usage of former times,
is requited by the same means, leaving the receiver
the choice of all the productions of nature or art,
either for necessity or enjoyment, and rendering
him consequently far more independent of his em-
ployer, than any other consideration for his labour
could do — it is of the greatest importance, particularly for the bulk of the labouring classes, that
too sensible a scarcity of coin do not take place,
which, with a weighty standard, and the precious metals being high in price, must necessarily
happen; whereby the daily and weekly circulation
would be impeded, and it would be impossible to
obtain with facility, those quantities of the necessities or comforts of life, which are required for daily
consumption. — It is only since money has circulated in such abundance, as to afford the means of
universal exchange, and of satisfying every species
of service, in its smallest ramifications, that the
division of labour has so wonderfully progressed

through which alone, the present prosperity of manufactories and fabrics, and the perfection of their
productions, could have been attained; every stoppage in this main spring, would cause a retrograde
movement in the animated transactions of civil society, or even bring them to a total ttagnation.

The simularity of the intimate connexion, which
exists between all the European states, will exempt
none of them from a bankruptcy, of the nature we
have above described, as s o o n a s t h e n e c e s s i t y
s h a l l a p p e a r o f s u c h t a k i n g p l a c e i n
t h a t c e n t r a l p o i n t o f E u r o p e a n t r a f f i c,
where the greatest load of debt exists, be it in government paper or a representative currency, which
can alone be liquidated by the precious metals; and
the most powerful remedy against the inconvenien-
ces attendant upon such a measure, and the hope
of all inequalities being levelled in the shortest manner to reciprocal satisfaction, are to be found in
this very universality of the case. For if it were
possible to suppose, that in a considerable state
of great influence, the value of merchandize, to that
of gold and silver, could remain at the same standard, when in all other countries on account of the
want of bullion, it had already fallen the half or
more, it must then be allowed, that as long as this
continued, the intercourse with the former country
would be broken off. For as all trade grounds

itsesf on the principle, that the seller can again purchase his productions and wares, at the same price
he disposed of them for, which is nothing further,
than repaying the labour of the producer and manufacturer, and moreover be able to gain what may be
necessary for his own support, during the interval
of the exchange, the state, in which the ancient
relative value still existed, must necessarily keep its
export articles too high in price, and the other countries, where the quantity of precious metal demanded, would pay for double the labour, would not
have it in their power to pay the price required by
the former. But the impossibility of things remaining in this condition for a continuance, appears
evident; for the precious metals would soon wander
from those states, where they were equivalent to the
smallest quantity of labor and produce, into those,
where they could pay for more; and this exportation — in spite of all imaginable obstacles — would
continue to flow, until the quantity of bullion became equally distributed over all those territories,
united by, or accessible to a reciprocal commerce,
and the relative value of produce and merchandize,
had once more found its level.

If it would not appear too bold to cherish the
hope, that in the same laudable manner, in which
the several governments have commenced to reconcile the external relations of their different states,

by friendly agreements, they would equally be inclined to submit the internal affairs of their countries, in as far as regarded the important interests
of the whole, to a general discusion, it might reasonably be expected, that the regulation of the relative value of money, would become a topic of deliberation, as the continually encreasing distraction
of the finances of all, would stimulate each individually to bring this subject upon the carpet. A measure of this nature is the only one capable of giving birth to, a uniformity of the pecuniary standard
throughout Europe, so suitable to the occasions of
the age; which amongst all institutions, would unquestionably be the most important, that a truly
paternal care could employ, for the alleviation of
commerce, and the prevention of manifold obstacles
and frauds, and which would of itself as it were,
call to light a u n i f o r m s c a l e, of all local weights
and measures.

But however important this solicitude may be,
and however applicable it may appear to measures,
excellent for the community at large, on a reciprocal understanding having taken place, the more
each government individually, must prevent, by
every exertion of state - policy, and the most disinterested sacrifice of self - interest, a real baukruptcy
taking place, incalculable in its injurious consequences, instead of that nominal one, which according to

our humble calculation, may be considered as the
minimum of an inevitable evil. It is evident from
this antithesis, that under a r e a l bankruptcy, we
mean that state of things, in which the government
finds itself no longer able, to fulfil the t r u e value
of its engagements, by paying so much in money,
as would purchase the same quantity of produce or
wares, which could have been bought, by the legal
sums due to the state-creditor, before the rise in
value of the precious metals took place, and whereby, the income of those, whose existence depends
on services rendered and capitals advanced the state,
must consequently be curtailed. Symtoms precede
this state-bankruptcy, which, as warning presages
merit every attention, appearing to announce a partial bankruptcy, in the several relations of the respective classes, of civil society. A token of this
kind is, that nothwithstanding the emigrations of
labourers, for the last eight or ten years, and although no local fall but even a rise in the price of
provisions has taken place, the weavers wages, according to the latest and best authorities, have fallen in
the manufacturing towns of England, in the short
space of two years, and in many cases within nine
months, to the half of what they amounted to, where
the highest, and have been reduced a quarter where
the lowest payment was given; the price of other

species of labour has also sunk in like proportion *),
The manufacturing districts of other states, where
the workman with wife and children and a bleeding
heart, is obliged for want of the means of daily subsistence to forsake his home and country, present a
no less gloomy prospect. Let this actual state of things,
which we have discussed more at large in the VIth
chapter, arise either from a too extensive production, disproportioned to the possible means of sale
for the articles produced, whereby their price becomes depressed, and the master manufacturer obliged to secure his diminished profit, by lowering the
price of labour, or from an excess of competition in
the number of hands seeking employment in this
branch of industry, (which would imply a want of
other channels for the employment of activity)
whereby the master in enabled to reduce the price
of wages to the lowest limits, or from both these
causes uniting to produce the melancholy result;
that nation nevertheless, considered in the light of
a social body, is already to be looked upon as i n s o l-
v e n t, who can no longer satisfy the claims of its

---

*) The Börsen Halle newspaper No. 2190 for 1819
    contains a specification of wages in Manchester,
    borrowed from the Times, which fully warrants
    the above result.

different members on the public income, the amount of the general gain being no longer adequate to the support of the community. — It will not do to object, that this common revenue is too unequally divided, and that the phenomenon in question, is to be attributed to such unequal distribution; for in whatever hands the income may be, it is, in regard to its circulative powers, completely the same, as it again streams out from every hand in exchange for necessities and luxuries of all descriptions, and for this reason may be considered, in its totality, as a river in constant motion; that is to say, provided it be not hoarded up, and thereby cause a sensible stagnation, which appearance of a universal want of credit, would be the approaching symptom of a complete dissolution. The present impossibility of keeping the wages of the labouring classes in equilibrium, with the requisites for a tolerable existence, may rather be attributed most safely to a diminution of the national income, decreased at least relatively, to a population which has perhaps augmented beyond the usual progression. This explanation of the case, is completely confirmed by what we said above, respecting the consequences, which the independence of America will have for the European manufacturing and commercial system; for every progress that is made beyond the ocean, in producing and fabricating those articles necessary for the wants or

conforts of life, and which hitherto had been supplied from hence, causes one branch of European
industry to decay, and one of the numerous springs
to dry up, from which the public income flows together. The effects of this, must necessarily fall
back upon the labouring classes, as long as at least,
the main stock of general industry does not send
forth a new shoot in the place of the one that is
withered, and fresh sources be not opened to the
public revenue. But the more extensive, the navigation, the manufacturing industry and commercial traffic is, which Europe must shortly lose *);
the more difficult will it be, for even the most industrious people, to make amends for such loss, and
the longer the intervening period will be, before
the new springs of national wealth, which must then
be dug for deeper, will flow sufficiently abundant.
But as long as the national income is really diminished, and in a constant state of decline, the decrease of the real revenue of the government, which is nothing more than an aliquot part
of the national receipts, cannot fail to follow, but
will rather retrogade in proportion to the diminution of the former. For we may most assuredly
maintain without fear of contradiction, that in all

*) Look back at the VIIIth chapter.

the considerable states and communities of Europe,
that proportion of the united income, which is levied in taxes for the necessities of the state *), has
already experienced a tension so unnatural, that it
would be dangerous, if not impossible to strain it
higher, in order to produce a larger quotient. But
this quotient far from being able to be encreased, is
much rather liable to be considerably diminished,
provided the greater competition in the markets of
Europe, continues to depress the price of corn **)

*) To the direct taxes and imposts paid to the state
   are also to be added, the immense sums which
   are levied in all European states, for town and
   parish-dues, poor's-rates, support of hospitals and
   also what the equipment of the militia, burgh-
   er-guards, and other personal taxes cost the
   individual. To reduce the whole of these
   contributions, will constitute one of the
   most important cares of the several governments,
   if the principal intent of every state-union, the
   welfare of the subject, is not to be sacrificed to
   the exaction of these taxes.

                                    Author.

**) In the Edingburg review for January 1820, the
   editors not alone express their opinion, that the
   value of gold will rise, and that the prices of
   all other articles must still fall lower, as a
   consequence thereof, but that it will encrease
   the difficulty, of paying the nominal amount of

and the general distress frustrates the execution of legal measures, for keeping it up, as in England, at an unnatural high rate. The only possibility of augmenting this aliquot part on the one side in order to cover the inevitable deficiency on the other, is to encrease the number of contributors, by bringing those without employment, into a state of activity, thereby rendering them productive members of the community, and gradually drawing them within the verge of taxation; on which subject, we have thrown out some hints in the Xth chapter. But as experiments of this nature, do not proceed with rapidity, and cannot, at least in those states which hitherto derived their principal income from the European manufacturing and commercial systems, likeep pace, with its decrease; such countries are likely unavoidably to witness for a period of time, a considerable reduction in their revenue, which deficit will continue to grow more alarming. But upon the public receipts being diminished, and government possessing no resources to supply the deficiency, the necessity of a d e c r e a s e i n e x p e n d - i t u r e, follows of itself, and the question is only,

_____

the present heavy permanent taxes in Great Britain.

Translator.

how such can be brought about, and on whom it is to fall.

In all European countries, the public expenditure is divided into two very distinct classes, the one of which is dedicated to the maintenance ef the state machine, in its present organization, the other to the fulfilment of those engagements, which the state has contracted for its preservation, or other purposes, in past times, and left to posterity as a sacred debt, inseparable from the possessions transmitted them. Which of these two branches we examine, in order to discover the possibility of lessening the expenditure, and thereby preventing a complete rupture, or a public declaration of the state, acknowledging its inability to fulfill its engagements, and the necessity of arbitrarily reducing, if not, of wholly annulling them, we meet every where with the most insurmountable difficulties. If the present organization of political oeconomy is to continue, it becomes very difficult in the most states, to determine, where the restrenchment, which necessity imperiously demands, is to come from. The expences of the establishments, on which this oeconomy reposes, appear every where already, to have been reduced to their very extreme limits. The pay of the standing armies, the maintenance of the navies, the salaries of but too numerous officers of the state, who nevertheless can with difficulty keep our too - complicated state-machines in an unwieldy motion, the support requisite for the arts and sciences, and even the enormous, yet insufficient provision made in most countries for the poor — are, taken on an average, and turned into the material necessities of life, so disproportionately inadequate, that a considerable field must be left open, for illegal gain, such as the abuse of public monies, fees, bribes, and every description of fraud, in order to account for the possibility of many servants of government physically existing, which the lawful emoluments of their offices could on no account enable them to do. Under these circumstances, an encreased endowment for public services appears more necessary, than it is possible to imagine, or accomplish a retrenchment. And in this lays a very cooperating cause of the universal relaxation of those ties of esteem and attachment, which ought to unite the governed, to their authorities; in this, the hidden seed of an internal rancour, which could easily degenerate into open dissention; in this, a ground source of the moral depravity, complained of so universally, and pervading more and more the several classes of society. For the majesty of the throne being immediately inaccessible to the majority of the people, is, and ought to be rather viewed from a distance, as the most elevated object, than examined and comprehended by the subject on a nearer

inspection therefore its attributes and the effects of
its power, are divided, like the rays a single light,
and participated by the servants of its authority.
The armed force, is an emblem in the eye of the
people, of the power of the sovereign, affording protection to the good, and subduing the contumacy
of the bad; his justice beams from every tribunal,
which deals out the law in the name of him who is
invisible, but considered to be present; his paternal
care shews itself in the council where the interest of
the whole and the welfare of the common family,
are deliberated upon, and his determinations are
carried into effect, by the inferior authorities, who
are interspersed amongst the people. No human
power will be able to prevent the hidden archetype
from being compared to the image reflected in the
above mirrors. It must therefore necessarily tend
to weaken the social ties, and dissipate the veneration, due to power and supremacy, if the servants
of the state are looked upon in a bad or doubtful
light, or if they depart from that external propriety,
and dignity of their immediate sphere, which at all
times ought to distinguish them; but it is more de-
plorable, when led, through poverty and domestic
misery, they commit acts of public baseness; or their
indigence lowering them in the estimation of the
multitude, renders them the objects of the proud

(24)

pity of the wealthy citizen. Such is indeed the condition of things at present, that to devote one's self
to the service of the state, and to bring up the growing generation for the same purpose, unless under
peculiarly favorable circumstances, is a step which
requires the most mature consideration, through the
apprehension of not acquiring a decent maintenance,
imperiously necessary, and not to be rejected by even
the most disinterested mind. — As little favorable
impression does it make, when public works, such
as buildings, roads and canals remain unfinished,
or are carried on but slowly and imperfectly for
want of resources; and whenever the people, assembled together at public solemnities or festivities; feeling themselves as one body, and beholding their
own grandeur, in the splendor of their government,
as in a central mirror, ought to evince a joyful
interest on the occasion, poverty paralizes the springs
of action, and indigence is visible on every side
through borrowed glitter. We refrain from entering further into this subject, as from what has been
said, the result is sufficiently clear, that rather an
increase than a saving in the expenditure, may be
reasonably expected, if the engine of state is to be
maintained in its present organization.

If we direct our view to the other class of the
national expences, namely the providing for the interest of the funded, and the liquidation of the float-

ing public debt, it is evident, that no saving can take place here, by an arbitrary reduction of the rate of interest, without de facto declaring the bankruptcy of the state. And if even the utmost unavoidable distress, might excuse such a despotic stroke of power, at the moment of its execution, yet its consequences are of that serious nature, that a d i s c e r n i n g state-policy, would sacrifice every thing, rather than unconcerned allow, the possibility of this dangerous measure occurring at a future time, which would no longer be within its controul. For as has been observed above, the national debt in all its branches, forms amongst most nations, the income of a very considerable class, of citizens, of importance and great influence, by reason of the superiority of their wealth and education'; who, accustomed to no other means of acquirement, and confidently reposing their whole welfare on this alone, would bitterly feel the smallest curtailment of their income, and would loudly bewail seeing themselves, as a reward for their confidence, exposed to wretchedness, or at least to a state of poverty, the more sorrowfully contrasted with their former opulence. The fate of all charitable institutions, requires more seriously, to be taken into consideration; for on their unimpaired continuance, the last resource of so many helpless beings, particularly of the other sex, depends, which latter, less favorably gifted by nature, with the means of self-protection and unrewarded by the state, for the meritorious sacrifices they nothwithstanding make to the public welfare, grounded as this is, alone on domestic virtue, have in all ages justly excited the piety and tenderness of the benefactors of the human race, towards the foundation of suitable asylums for them. The funds of these and other philanthropic institutions originally indebted to private benevolence, are almost every where placed in the hands of government, partly in consequence of the natural confidence shewn to the state, as being considered the safest debtor, and partly agreable to hints and insinuations urged by those at the helm. These revenues now depend either on inscriptions in the great book of the public debt, on treasury bills, or on various descriptions of government paper, sanctioned by authority and under the guarantee of the country. Should these promissory engagements, by the inability of the state, lose their customary value, and be buried in the ruin of universal desolation, the prop of existing poverty and the hope of posterity falls to the ground; for what renewed support or assistance, has the latter to expect from an age like this, void of commiseration, and unmindful, in the ardent pursuit after uncertain gains, and ephemeral enjoyments, of its own, but how far more forgetful of the future welfare of posterity? — If we descend from the regard

of public institutions, to the private relations between man and man, which being founded under the
protection of the laws, on the confidence of the duration of the conditions and forms of reciprocal engagements, enacted and guaranteed by the government, de-
serve the most conscientious consideration; we are
likely to find there, a still stronger inducement, to
exert every means, of warding off if possible, the dreaded subversion of the public credit. For it is subject to
no doubt, that the example given by the state, of
annulling the legal obligations of debitor to creditor, will make its way into individual intercourse,
and there be attended with similar revolutions.
For with what kind of right, could that state,
which having arbitrarily reduced its capital debt a
third part, or having lowered the stipulated rate of
interest from 6 and 5 to 3 and 2 pro cent, exempt
itself, from allowing the private debtor to enjoy the
same indulgence at the hands of his creditor? — In
many cases pure justice could demand a similar
concession, at least for that class of state creditors,
who being indebted to private persons, and having
their incomes reduced by the above measure, could
not be required to pay their debtors a larger rate
of interest, than had been meted out to them by the
government. But not taking this particular view
of the case into consideration, the whole machinery
of civil society is so intimately connected, that the

greater must necessarily hurry along with it, the smaller integral parts, and one wheel forced from its position, must produce here a stoppage, and create there, an unnatural motion. Thus, what would be nothing more than strictly just for the state-creditors, would be but highly equitable on the other hand, for the multitude of those, who interwoven with this numerous class of consumers, and enjoying in daily circulation more or less the benefits of their income, would sensibly feel their own welfare injured by the diminished prosperity of their patrons. Nor is it upon the whole possible to be imagined, that a legal benefit could be conferred upon a particular class in the state, undistinguished by any peculiar marks of office or of honor, but merely grounded on the fluctuating possession of claims upon the government, without at the same moment extending it to all. But it is evident, how hard such a measure would fall upon the generality of creditors, what complaints it would engender, and what an infinity of contrary claims, differences, and public law-suits, it would occasion. For if even, when viewed on the whole, we find that the qualities of debtor and creditor are not so distinct in individuals, but that many if not the majority unite both in their own persons, whereby the injustice done on the one side, would appear to be compensated by the indulgence shewn on the other; yet, in the infinite number of particular cases, this often does not occur, or only partially and imperfectly. Moreover, a doubtful interpretation of the law, with its whole train of distraction, reciprocal animosities, and just complaints, not so easily to be relieved, will shake the foundation of all social union, if mine and thine no longer repose upon ancient good-faith, and acknowledged laws, but are to be subdivided afresh according to a reduced scale, resting wholly on Convenience, a right hitherto unacknowledged. — Under circumstances of such pecuniary derangement, the possession and value of land and other immoveable property, would be subjected to great change and lamentable fluctuation. For in the course of time, and through the great intricacy of the social ties, it has happened, that only few landed estates belong wholly or unreservedly to their possessors; the most are, if examined, divided between these, and men of capital, in the quality of mortgagees. The latter, commonly spleculators of foresight, and inactive spectators, are better able to judge of the course of events, than the industrious class of citizens and agriculturists; and in distracted times, pregnant with changes and reductions, they will at all events seek to secure themselves by calling in their capitals with the least possible loss, as long as there is yet time, in order to be enabled to profit more advantageously of circumstances. This

tendency acted upon generally, will render it impossible for the land owners to pay back their mort-
gages as required by their creditors; for money being
in request from all sides, no one will feel inclined,
under the above state of things, to part with it. The
last melancholy resource of publicly selling the
estates at any price, must as long as this crisis continues, reduce their relative, far below their actual
or productive value; speculation will possess itself
of immoveable, as if it were moveable property, in
order to resell to a profit tomorrow, what had been
purchased yesterday. Under a continued repetition
of ephemeral possessors, the love of the soil, and
with it the care of its cultivation, the attachment of
the tenants, and every remnant of those moral ties,
which raised the true nobleman and the independent landholder to a patriarch within his own boundaries, and to the most loyal vassal of his king and
country, must vanish; and in the place of that spirit, which is bent on preserving and protecting paternal property received in descent from honorable
ancestors, mean interestedness, and the most contemptible dissipation, which fells the tree, in order
to enjoy its fruit the more promptly and with less
labour, will appear.

Such has been the the condition of things in all
ages, when bad internal oeconomy, and a too great
distention of its external relations, have exhausted

the resources of the state, and have rendered it incapable, of maintaining the balance between the claims
of subsistence, and the means of satisfying them.
And how reasonable is it not, to apprehend the
appearance of this situation, at no very distant period, on the overgrown system of European politics,
and commercial supremacy falling to the ground;
when this overthrow will threaten to lead back our
quarter of the globe to an internal oeconomy, suitable to its extent and proportionate to its natural
resources? —

Were it possible to produce a conviction in the
minds of those, who are possessed of power and the
means of decision, or of those, whose duty it is immediately to influence the former, that on our inac-
tively giving ourselves up to the course of time, a
state; such as we have described above, actually
impends over our heads; then the hope would undoubtedly yet remain, that a vigorous determination; quickly adopted by the government, would
enable it to maintain the helm, and by consider-
ately meeting, and systematically acting upon the
revolution of things, once become inevitable,
would prevent the suddeness of the change, hinder
the chaotic distraction of the transition, and deprive
the new social formation, from bearing the stamp
of a revolutionary origin; which indiscriminately

confounds justice with injustice. If, as we have endeavored to shew, there is no prospect of reestablishing the balance in the income and expenditure of
the most European states, on their retaining their
present political organization, (and which we have
taken for granted), then, no other remedy can be
applied, but to make a timely and voluntary
renunciation of the existing institutions,
and with wise circumspection and vigorous hand,
even to proceed to the formation of new ones. Did
the inclination once shew itself of being willing to
change the system; the special knowledge of its present organization, and the particular character and
nationality of each people and country, would dis-
tinctly point out, what should be rejected, what
should be admitted, and according to what principles, the old institutions could be united with the
new. We can only trace out here, those prominent
features in the imperfections of the times, which
developing themselves, with or without our interference, cannot be pernicious and irregular, but in
the latter case.

It will be necessary probably in the first place,
to limit that principle, hitherto supported from so
many sides, and agreable to which, the power of
government, extending a leading influence into the
smallest ramifications of society, stands ruggedly
opposed to the people, being those who are governed,

and also to invalidate the maxim, which centres the administration of the state, exclusively in a class of persons in its pay, being considered as a thing wholly incompatible with the properties of a citizen in his quality of subject. — There, where the man defends himself, is to be found the protector, and where he conducts his own affairs, there is no need of an administrator. And it is subject to no doubt, but that a great part of that, which is done for the people at present, by means of a number of functionaries who are paid for the purpose, could be executed without salary, just as well, and even better, by the people themselves, provided they were gradually attracted by political institutions to afford local assistance, and administer themselves, their own affairs.

That by training the whole male population of a nation to the use of arms, which we have recommended elsewhere in another point of view, and which in opposition to the standing, might be termed the sedentary army of the country, the state would annually save large sums *), is very evident,

---

*) From a sketch drawn in the Political Journal for 1818, (V. I. P. 127) it many be seen in what proportion, the army expences stand to the state revenue, and according to which the income of

nor will it be disputed, that the allurements for war,
and the temptation of invading the rights of a
weaker neighbour must cease, with the unfortunate
facility of leading an army completely equipped
into the field, and at the same time, the former occasion of the encrease of the public debt. But as ancient, as well as the most modern history sufficiently
shew the possibility, of the citizen being formed
into a defender of the common soil, and into a powerful protector and avenger of the national honor,
so do they in like manner, present us with excellent
examples, of his being equally useful and capable
of participating in the administration of the common
affairs, for which he must feel the deepest interest,
if it only be the serious intention of the government,
to call upon him for this purpose. It is our opinion
therefore, that as an attention to the whole, particularly in regard to the general security, the administration of justice, and the defence of the
country, is the incumbent duty of the government,
on the other hand, the administration of all local

the Prussian monarchy, is estimated at 48 millions of dollars, of which 22 are required for the
maintenance of the standing army. Nor is this
expence likely to be diminished, if the present
system is to be continued.

and special interests ought, without the least hesitation to be left to the different communities, as being the nearest concerned, if only care were taken, that by an energetic and proper subordination of the several powers — which the French term Hiérarchie des pouvoirs — individual ebullitions did not derange the motion of the whole. — According to this principle, every sort of local police, all correctional-jurisdiction, the maintenance of public buildings, harbours, and caritable institutions, as well as the support of the poor, as matters irrelevant with the higher duties of the government and its finances, would be confidently entrusted to the care of the different communities, as was formerly and is in several places, the case now. Also the distribution of the taxes to be levied on the people for the necessities of the state, and the expences of local oeconomy, would be effected much better by means of representatives chosen from amongst them, than by the delegates of government, who are generally ignorant of the ability and the means of contribution peculiar to different individuals; but it is a matter of course, that government should constantly retain a controul over embezzlement and fraud, and a power of decision in cases of dispute, and complaints of partiality and unjust proceedings, on the part of the local authorities and overseers. The government being freed, by these and similar dispositions, from a multitude of partial cares and anxieties, not belonging to its province, and being exalted above all petty detail, would be able to grasp the reins of the whole, with a more vigorous hand, and would gain in proportion in moral grandeur and in the veneration of the people. By mixing itself less in the affairs and private actions of individuals, it would shew itself, when it was necessary so to do, with all the majesty of the throne, in order, more energetically to enforce that obedience and respect, which is due to the sovereign by the subject, and which nothing weakens more, than the interference of government in relative matters of little consequence, where wrong measures are for the most part infallibly adopted, through the natural ignorance of the local merits of the case. For it is with the state, in this, as with the oeconomy of the individual, in which the head of the family is looked upon in a contemptible light, who instead of employing himself in the preservation and the increase of the joint property, and retaining the principal management of the whole, directs his attention to the detailed concerns of the house, which he will never be able to understand so well, as those who have been ordained by nature to attend to these duties. By a change of this nature, the several communities would also be gainers; directly, by the less expence of a voluntary administration, and

still more indirectly, by the more assiduous attention they whould pay to their own, rather than to
the concerns of their neigbours; the citizen and the
inhabitant of the country would look upon his town
or district as his property, and would watch over
its interests, as soon as he was indulged with a suitable share in the deliberations of its administration.
The government on the other hand, would reap the
infinite advantage, of being able to dedicate itself
exclusively to the care of the whole, which it
alone comprehends and is alone called upon to regulate, by passing over particularities, and all matters of detail, which it is still unable, entirely to
fathom.

And what a multitude of important objects, de-
manding the most undivided solicitude, do not present themselves in this sphere of its deliberations;
particularly at a time, agitated by an indeterminate
fermentation, in which so much that is new and uncommon, impetuously bursts forth, and which must
be ordered and adjusted, if the whole, forced from
its ancient course, and finding no new level, shall
not to sink in indiscriminate ruin ! Here we direct
our view principally to the consolidation and establishment of representative constitutions, s u c h a s
h a v e l a t e l y b e e n a g a i n i n t r o d u c e d, in
France, the Netherlands, Poland and in different
German states, or, s u c h a s a r e s t i l l t o b e

formed, agreable to received assurances, in many other parts of the German confederation and we conceive, we are not hazarding too much in asserting, that it will be the most difficult problem for the art of government, to lead the nations through the transition of the old into a new existence, without incurring dangerous commotions. For every animated power, once put in motion, goes irresistably forwards, if an adequate counterpoise be not opposed to it; and according to this law, as several symptoms of the times seem also to attest, nothing is to be apprehended more, than that in states, in which the people have been called to a participation in the government, never before exercsied, the principles of monarchy are likely to be thrown too much into the shade, and their energy weakened, by the intrusion of maxims, designated democratic. But no greater misfortune could befal Europe, than the elements of monarchy being paralyzed, which alone correspond with the ancient manners and customs of her nations, and are at the same time capable of preserving their unity, and political existence *). But if this sublime end of all

---

*) The nature of the case must convince the more thoughtful observer, that the young states of America cannot be held up, as an example proving

national welfare is to be attained, the government must above all things, exercise the greatest precaution in making those advances towards a reform, which we have considered necessary, and in resigning that which is no longer tenible, in order to prevent what is justly demanded, and has been granted with disinterested generosity, being impetuously laid claim to, and violently seized on, whereby no limits would be foreseen to the demands on the one, and concessions on the other side !

Scarcely less difficult, does the situation of governments appear, in those states, where as in Great Britain, by reason of constitutions, of long standing, old abuses, or imperfect guarantees for their supposed rights, claim the anxious attention of the people, on account of the universal tendency to innovation, and the uncomfortable state of their present existence, cramped on so many sides. The government must here strive, above all, to uphold the fundamental pillars of the edifice, but to reconstruct in a manner suitable to the necessities of the age,

---

the practical possibility of the total abolition of monarchial principles in Europe; the result of the attempts made to imitate the above pattern, may serve as instruction to the more sanguine!

(26)

those of its ancient compartments, which no longer
afford their inhabitants security or convenience.
But, to prevent a general state-bankruptcy, with all
the ruinous consequences, we have already pictured,
no more powerful remedy presents itself, than in
those countries, where a national representation is
embodied to deliberate on the affairs of the community, to determine by well-appointed regulations,
the share such assembly shall have, in the administration of the finances. For since that nice confidence is now lost, which, upon the model of a happy
family, peaceably entrusted the affairs of the community, to the direction of the highest authority,
without mutually binding themselves by irksome
conditions; if the age, and the restless spirit of aggrandizement, and an unnatural distension of the
resources of the state, have created difficulties no
longer to be solved in the usual manner, and as the
right of a joint deliberation has been granted to
the people, there is undoubtedly no subject that
calls for a more important exercise of this invalu-
able prerogative, than that, which concerns that
share of income, the community at large and each
individual, are called upon by the state, to contribute towards its necessities and the public welfare.
If even a total reform in the present features of administration and the existing system, were inevitable, if even, here or there, a reduction of the national

debt, were the only means of giving birth to a better order of things, it would be effected under a representative constitution, not without considerable public and private distraction, but yet without producing those consequences, which under other circumstances, such decisive measures would most probably develope.

XII.

In the former chapter, we have closely investigated the effects of the entire independence of America, on the pecuniary and financial system of Europe, and find as the results of our enquiry, that the consequent decrease of the precious metals in circulation, on the one part, is likely to enhance their intrinsic value, which would occasion the establishment of a new pecuniary standard; whereas, on the other hand, the stagnation of commerce, and the inactivity of those branches of industry, deprived of the usual transatlantic vent for their productions, would effect a diminution in the national income; this decrease in the receipts of the country would cause a deficit in the usual revenues of government, and the embarassment in covering it, would tend above all, to pave the way for the introduction of new forms both political and administrative; the expenditure of the states would at all events be lessened; the present expedient of obtaining resources, by continually augmenting the national debt, abolished; and the existing load of the public engagements, would be reduced proportionably to the new order of things, even at the risk of being attended with a state-bankruptcy. What change these antecedents are likely to occasion in civil life, and in the influence exercised by the different classes of society on each other, and what alteration they may produce in the course of time, in national characer, manners and modes of living, shall at present form the objects of our consideration.

Europe, deprived of her most important colonies, and carrying on with difficulty a contest against the encreasing preponderance of America, for the preservation of the remainder, probably fruitless in the long-run, will become poorer; she will have no equivalent to offer that quarter of the globe, no longer standing in need of her natural and manufactured commodities, for that mass of productions she has hitherto been in the habit of drawing from thence, and must consequently renounce generally, if not wholly, the use of

such *). Industry hitherto directed to objects of foreign commerce, will turn its attention to the

---

*) We find a remarkable confirmation of this pro-
position in the following article taken from the
Börsen - Halle newspaper of 4th Novbr. 1819.

"In the latest work of Mr. von Humboldt,
"there is a calculation of the immense sums;
"which go from Europe so inconsiderable in
"size, to America and Asia, not for necessi-
"ties of life, but for articles we could fully
"do without. Who would have supposed,
"that we use annually 140 millions of lbs of
"coffee, 32 millions lbs. of tea, of which ⅔ds
"remain in England, 32 millions lbs. of co-
"coa, and 450 millions lbs. of sugar? These
"articles looked upon by us as indispensible,
"swallow up yearly 558,200,000 Franks. The
"industry of Europe is inadequate to supply
"an exchangeable value in merchandize, equal
"to the amount of this enormous consump-
"tion, whence follows, that gold and silver
"lose themselves in Asia and come out of
"circulation in Europe. Under- the above
"558 millions of francs, which sugar, coffee,
"tea and cocoa, cost, the value of dye-woods,
"spices, diamonds, pearls, cotton &c. &c. is
"not reckoned."

The author has not hitherto seen the work, from
which, this information is derived.

native soil, ¶n order to win from it reparation for those privations which threaten to be felt more sensibly, from day to day. The distress of a population becoming continually more dense, and violently contending with the means of existence, which the resources of the state founded on an artificial organization, have no longer the means of alleviating, being felt by all, will call forth those inherent animated powers, whose friction will destroy the mechanical and passive mode of thinking, hitherto pursued, which takes no interest in all, that does not come in immediate contact with physical welfare. Man does not voluntarily forsake the course he has been accustomed to move in, but on being forced into a sphere of new activity, he will gradually gain strength in contending with unwonted difficulties. The mind will be unable to direct itself so decidedly as at present, to gain and the acquirement of immense riches; other and more honorable roads to celebrity, will present themselves; the spirit of speculation will be limited, but a greater fund of labour will await us, and a more multilateral activity will summon the Citizen to more general duties, and render him partaker of a more enlightened state of culture. Possessed of fewer pecuniary means, and having less time for enjoyment, man will no longer consider it, indispensible for his existence, but will become more moderate in his wants,

and more p o l i t i c in the noblest Grecian sense of
the word; with this quality, sentiments of respect
and consideration, which his sphere of action will
command from his fellow-citizens, will indemnify
him for a thousand vanities, which are only of value, when d i g n i t y is not to be attained, by any
other means. Thus then the ideas of h o n o r and
d i s t i n c t i o n would in the first place, be subject
to other modifications, and a wider field would be
opened to emulation, than the service of court or
state in its more confined sense, has hitherto been
able to hold out. The ideas also of the extent of
knowledge, necessary for the general improvement
of all, from the highest to the lowest independent
citizen in the state, and the direction, which e d u-
c a t i o n must take, in order to stimulate individual
activity amongst the various classes of people, will
experience a visible change.

In conjunction with the elementary rudiments,
on which the acquirement of knowledge is alone
founded, religion has hitherto been the only subject, of which some instruction, has been given to
all without exception; but for the future, the study
of native objects, the constitution of his country,
and the essential ideas of the laws, to which the citizen is amenable, will form a cycle of universal
information, which will be foreign to none, whose
pretentions place them above the menial classes

In this circle of civic knowledge and its exercise in political life, the man of letters cannot but come in friendly contact with the industrious burgher, the clergy with the laity, the man of business with the artist, and the citizen with the well-informed country-man. The service of arms, on the duties of the militia being no longer confined to a particular class, but undertaken by the body of the citizens, to whom they essentially belong, will constitute another circle of social approximation and generous emulation. Without doubt it becomes every man, and belongs to a just idea of his perfection, to be able to guard and protect his life and property, and with the same power and ability, to defend the existence and honor of his country, against attack and violation. The preparatory exercise necessary for the fulfilment of these duties, has almost every where been viewed hitherto, as a forced or remunerated service, to evade which, has been looked upon as an advantage and a privelege, but on no account as a voluntary duty, incumbent on the citizen himself, and to withdraw himself from which, would be considered disgraceful. But this will be different for the future, and the youths of all ranks, the flower of the whole nation, without regard to particular destinations, will assemble round the standard of their conntry, and having completed their exercise of arms, will meet from time to

time for purposes of discipline, should even the repose of their country be undisturbed. This armed
association, will most assuredly call to light, a spirit of harmony, an exchange of sentiments and feelings, and a love of the people amongst themselves,
incapable of being manifested at the present day;
for our children find only comrades at school, our
youth, companions, behind the counter, in public-
offices, the universities, or in the confined circle of
a garrison acquaintance! — The knowledge of the
use of arms, seems not to be acquired, and the exercise of them, not to be put into temporary practice,
without robbing the initiation of the youth in his
future vocation, and the actual employment of the
man in his particular occupation, of a portion of
time, which many would perhaps consider more
advantageously devoted to the latter objects; we
could be content with answering, that secondary
things must ever yield to those of a more important
nature, and that individual inclination, must model and accommodate itself to that, which the spirit of the times now renders inevitable, but in order to satisfy those, who are not so easily contented
with general refutations, we will combat the objec-
tion in detail.

In the first place it must be admitted, that a
variety of occupations, appears to generate the

(27)

necessary time required for them; and that those have usually the least, and are the latest finished, who without intermission, remain at the same uniform, and often unimportant employment. If so, it cannot be denied, that a healthy robust and active body, is undoubtedly rendered more vigorous, by the exercise in question, which will also promote the strength and ability of the mind, and consequently the time devoted to the use of arms, will easily be regained by the dispatch of a more sprightly activity; lastly, that the energies of the citizen, being directed to different objects, which engross the extent of his understanding, is a thing highly suitable to, and which becomes him as a Man, necessarily forming his mind in a stronger and more manly mould, and rendering him by these means, better qualified for his particular destination. Now, what is admitted in general, must also hold good in special cases. If we turn to the most numerous class of the people, which comprehends those, who derive principally their support from bodily labour and dexterity, we can conveniently divide them, into such as are employed in continual motion, and into such, as lead a sedentary life, dedicating themselves to the exercise of mechanical occupations. The use of arms, in as far as it affords the opportunity of being trained, from time to time in the open air, cannot but be beneficial to both; to the former,

because they will gain the strength necessary for
their laborious employments, and will become more
regular and more adroit, as the example of the pea
sants' sons who are enrolled in the standing armies,
clearly proves; to the latter, because the body,
which by a continued sedentary posture becomes
unbent and mollified, will find motion and a new
stimulus, in the above exercise. But with regard to
the attention to civic duties, and the execution of
public affairs, in as far as such could fall to the lot of
the parents and foremost members of this portion of
the people; the labouring classes, must be in a de-
plorable state, if the time employed in these engagements, would fall heavy upon the otherwise industrious citizen, and not rather be advantageous to
the prosecution of his occupation, by reason of this
very species of activity promoting the enlargement
of the understanding and creating a reciprocal exchange of ideas *). It will also be acknowledged
at last, and implanted in the worldly course of things,
that man shall labour in order to support life, but not
that life exists, for the sake of labour; an idea, which
once grown practical, must bring back to a more

---

*) The introduction of the new city - regulations in
Prussia, is not said to have produced injurious
consequences,

equitable scale, the striking disproportion, which is
found between labour and wages, particularly in the
branches of manufacturing industry. — If we pass on
to the mercantile class, as the mediator between
the ranks of society devoted to corporeal or intellectual labour, we shall also find, that neither the study, nor the use of arms, would be detrimental to the
young commercial pupil, as little as the exercise of
public charges and representative functions, would
be unsuitable for the merchant of consideration.
Further, if we regard the so-called learned order
in the state, the far more numerous portion of this
class, stand undoubtedly in need of a learned education, as necessary for the fulfilment of their
vocations, but are not destined to prosecute it further, or to enlarge the regions of science, being
only required to be acquainted with their existing
dimensions, and to put the results of this knowledge into practice, be it as servants of the church,
or of the law, of the administration or of public
oeconomy, or in the capacity of physicians and sur-
geons. Living amongst the people, they ought to
devote their whole time and attention to them, and
nothing can be more important, than to make themselves early acquainted with all their wants, and
throwing aside all higher notions of distinction, to
assimulate themselves, by experience, to their sentiments and character, and to shew them in every

thing which becomes the independent citizen of a
state, a noble and laudable example. Since it has
been looked upon as an advantage in our improved
public schools, that boys of very different ranks of
life, pass them in joint emulation in one common
course of instruction· and amusements; how much
greater must the benefits be, which the youths are
likely to reap in body as well as mind, by a general armed association, assembled round the standard of their country, for the purposes of exercise or
actual warfare, and which advantages must be imparted to the riper men, by being made participa-
ters in the affairs of the nation, either in the public
character of jurors , or as administrators of the city
or provincial revenues. But then the system of education would require a direction being given to it,
conformable to the object in view; above all, the
arts of oratory , formerly of such powerful weight,
must again be called into notice; it would be necessary to enrich the encyclopedia of knowledge
with many new branches, but to lopp off those, no
longer in unison with the necessities of the age. By
these means, which we particularly request, may
not be lost sight of, that, would take place voluntarily, agreable to the choice and dispositions of
those, to whom the direction of these objects might
be entrusted, which necessity will shortly of
itself bring about. For we dare to make the heretical

prophecy, that it will soon be impossible to retain the whole extent of bibliographical knowledge, required at present of those, who esteem themselves belonging, to the class of the learned; the very simple reason is, that this amplitude continually encreases with the progress of time, and ancient theories, being exploded by modern discoveries, must cease to be practical. The state of science, in all those branches adapted to common life, affords the most striking verification of this.

If henceforth, as is at present every where the case in Europe, the lawyer is to ground his jurisprudence, upon the knowledge of the detail of the Roman law, on the universal and particular rights and statutes of his own country, and the infinite number of the special ordinances and decrees of his government, it will not be possible, for youth to wind themselves, through the intricacies of such a voluminous study, which even now, almost exceeds their ability. The consequences are, that the memory is overloaded at the expence of the more exalted oversight and the power of judgment; and the application of the law becomes continually more difficult, by the doubtful nature of what is right, whereas the grand aim, of making their own laws intelligible to the people, becomes every day, less and less attainable. — It will be equally impossible for the future ecclesiastic, to find his proper place,

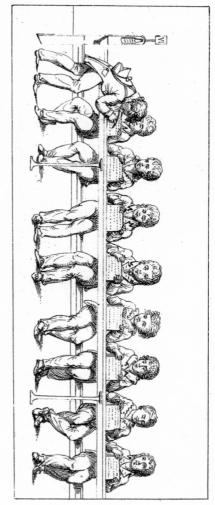

Mutual instruction in a Danish school

Manpower in a Danish cloth mill

from amongst the labyrinths of antiquated church and heretical legends, and the infinite apparatus of dogmatical and oriental erudition, comprehended under his preparatory studies, and to render what he has so laboriously acquired, of benefit to men as they now are, provided he shall suit the present necessities of the age, and be the guardian, the publisher and interpreter of those holy laws which are imprinted in the heart, which superior to all literal constructions, unite mankind in love and hope, and alone are capable of reestablishing the tottering pillars of the social union, and of reanimating those feelings for morality and decency, which have been deadened by the enormities of an age, without parallel. But the science of medicine, appears to be more in its infancy, than any other branch of human knowledge; being founded on the newer systems of anatomy and chemistry, it is likely, by the discovery of the magnetic and electrical powers, to be more and more led over, into the regions of physics and psychology; the physician who wishes to cultivate these sublime fields of intelligence with success, will find it unnecessary to burthen himself with the acquirement of more ancient theories, no longer possessing a practical influence in life. — That which is required, as an indispensible condition of a learned acquaintance with every branch of history, is also likely to be measured upon another scale very shortly. For the course of the world carries with it daily, its texture of events, and will render it impossible, at least for him, who cannot exclusively devote his whole life to this enquiry, to embrace a knowledge of the almost innumerable occurrences of modern times, with those of remoter ages, connected only with the present, by indistinct and almost imperceptible clews. Further, the more the world presses forward to a perfect state of unison, the more the knowledge and use of the modern languages will become necessary, as the means of reciprocal information and active cooperation; but the extensive study of the dead languages, now looked upon as the basis of academical knowledge for every person, will on this account be less cultivated, and subject to limitations. As belonging peculiarly to the province of history, it will without doubt be classed under this branch of science, as soon as the sources of positive knowledge can be derived from judicial books and scientific works, written in the languages of the existing countries *). Greece produced leaned men, in the true sense of the word, who understood no language but their own. —

---

*) It is a fortunate circumstance, that the mot important of the ancient languages, the Greek, by

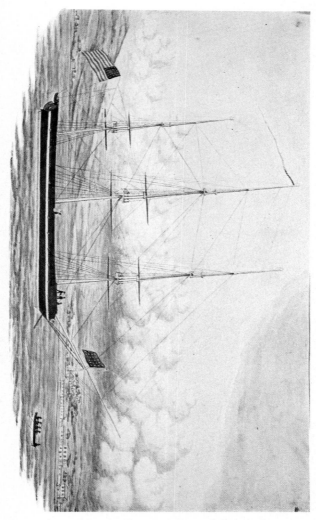

*The American Frigate Ontario anchored off the city of Smyrna (Izmir)
on the Turkish Mediterranean coast, 1825*

The Acropolis in Athens

Comanche Chasing Buffalo With Bows and Lances

In taking this view of the subject, how shall we be able to preserve the integrity of the sciences, which alone depends on the developement of the elementary ideas, or to maintain the connexion of the whole, reposing upon the occurrences of former times; and lin one word, how shall we be able to save the history of mankind from oblivion, which should unite the remotest with the most modern æras, by means of comprehensible transitions, and putting time out of the question, should reflect the picture of one infinite scene of life? We answer, this will happen in future, as has hitherto been the case, through those contributors to human knowledge and those masters in the fields of science, the l e a r n e d, in the proper acceptation of the word. We by no means wish to see this class, which is eminently important for mankind, and in certain respects the most honorable of all, assume an inferior station in society, but only more dis-

----

the course of events, as hinted at in the Xth chapter, will again perhaps, at no very great distance of time, be introduced generally into political life, whereby the knowledge and the use of the treasures contained in it, will be more universally dispersed.

tinctly separated than hitherto, from that of p r a c-
tical professors of the sciences. There
will, and must be in all ages, learned men; but
all those, who mean to devote themselves to a practical life, shall not be educated as such, for by this,
they often lose sight of the immediate present existence and its claims upon mankind; moreover, the
encreasing mass of the sciences, will alone render
the universality impossible, to which our literary
ostentation at the present day, but too eagerly as-
pires. But the true man of learning, should at least
be able to take a general survey of the whole of human knowledge, and be familiar with its threads, in
order to guide himself at pleasure through the mazes
of the mighty labyrinth, and devote himself to the
cultivation of some particular branch of science.
Being the guardian and adviser of the human race,
it is but reasonable, he should be held in distin-
guished estimation, and exempted for the future,
from civil burthens, in order to be enabled, free
from care, and earthly solicitudes, to soar aloft, and
abide in the spiritual regions of thought, and to fa-
shion with immaculate purity, those moulds, in which
the terrestrial substance ought to assume forms,
more worthy of the sublime image of humankind.
In the same parallel with the learned, stands the
artist, both representing the perfection of human
nature; it is the duty of each in his particular

sphere of action, to diffuse generally through actual
life, that nobleness, with which he has been inspired; on this account, both may claim equal privileges and exemptions in their respective paths, and
which can only appear without thorns to him, who
is unacquainted with the labours of the mind; the
palm however, should only be conferred on the
true man of learning, as on the real artist, (not
upon the mechanical imitator of master-pieces,
laying before him) and a preparatory school should
foster innate talent, and conduct it, with judicious
guidance to the distant, but exalted goal.

We have yet to speak of the nobility. This
class, originally representing those free by birth,
the peers of the sovereign, his natural counsellors
and companions in arms, in later ages denoted the
feoffees and large landed proprietors who often, in
contradiction to every idea of their estate, became
the opponents and assailants of the power and prerogatives of the crown, or acted as the tyrannical
oppressors of the lower classes of the people. Afterwards, being raised by the favor of the sovereign,
into an hereditary privileged caste, the majority of
the families composing it, were prefered, and even
exclusively appointed, to the higher offices of the
court and state; whereby no regard was paid to a
want of hereditary landed property, the possession of
which, originally constituted a necessary attribute,

of this order. If this class is to step forward with
any degree of weight, in the developement of the
new association of things every where on the eve of
taking place, and if it is to participate beneficially
in reordering the grand European constitution *),
it can only accomplish this object, by ardently asserting that character assigned it by nature, as mediator between the government and the people, and
supporter and protector of their existing rights,
instead of contenting itself with the enjoyment of
advantages and real or imaginary privileges; acting
thus nobly, it would form the dignified centre of
gravity, round which the reciprocal agitated powers
would assemble, and against which the unruly
waves of discord would break, which, without this
counterpoise, are not likely to be hushed with facility. In order fully to answer such a destination,
it would be absolutely necessary for the nobility
from their earliest youth, to be made acquainted
with, and love the country, which they are to defend, the constitution, which they are to support,
the rights of the different orders, which they are to
maintain, the laws, to which they are to enforce

---

*) It is known, that the element of nobility, has
not been admitted hitherto, into the American
constitutions.

obedience and respect, and to be brought up in every thing which is patriotic and national, educated amongst those, with whom, and for whom they are to live, and possess that courage and skill which become the future leaders of their countrymen in war, not less than that spirit for justice and undaunted integrity, which are disinterested guardians against oppression, and insurmountable barriers against the insolence of rebellious sedition. The true and only nobleman is regardless of himself in the welfare of the whole, and the lustre loses its dignity, if he, whom it distinguishes above so many, does not also accomplish, what so few are able to perform.

If we wished to draw, as it were, a perspective picture of the future state of Europe, agreable to the individual subjects of which we have treated, we ought above all things to determine the scale, upon which the value of this fleeting human life, and that of not less fleeting generations, is to be appreciated. He, who estimates life, according to the absence of uneasy and sorrowful feelings, or negative happiness, and according to a continuance and intensity of pleasant sensations, or positive enjoyment; he who prizes above every thing, the tranquillity and ease of an unimbittered existence, in possession of those benefits of life, the renunciation of which, our twofold nature painfully feels, and

which borrow from the force of habit, and the pre-
dilection of our forefathers, a double claim; lastly
he, who is anxious to reach the goal of life subject
to the least possible molestation, and rather bends
to the course of events, than actively puts his shoul-
der to the wheel of the times — will find this picture, provided he be able to survey it, from his point
of view, dismal and alarming in the extreme. For
most undoubtedly there will come a time of great
distress, and he who cannot submit to privations,
will sink; he who with self-denial and dependence
on himself, cannot support the exigency of the crisis,
will be hurried away in the vortex of universal affliction, and violently precipitated there, whither
he did not wish to go. There will probably be less
war, at least in the interior of Europe, if the powers, clinging, as they appear to do, to the idea of
an Areopagus to adjust their own differences, procure
it a lasting influence for the future; but storms
generated from the conflict of political elements,
and as much from national as individual oeconomical distress, will rage the more numerous, and
more dangerous. The continual decrease of the
means of subsistence, with which we are daily more
alarmingly threatened, is likely, with an encrease
of population, to plunge thousands of generations
otherwise blooming, into the vortex of misery, as
long as no remedy be applied, by a proper organization

of emigrations to foreign parts of the globe, or the settlement of colonists in the interior of Europe, on new lands. Despair may probably call to light, a series of sanguinary and cruel abominations, the hor. rible prelude to which, has already made its public appearance. A cry of constitutional reform, and an ungovernable striving and longing after new political codes, caused principally by the pressure of the times, and sensibly felt by all, are likely to shake the internal structure of more than one state, and to burst into the pernicious flames of civil discord; unless, the inordinate impetuosity of despotic power, or of popular capriciousness, be not driven back, within the pale of legality, by a wise conciliation of reciprocal claims, and determined perseverance in what is right, which must instil respect into the most untractable minds. Finally, that luxury, which has been nourished by the tribute of the usurp- ed dominion of the world, and the habitual extra- vagance in internal oeconomy, and external osten- tation, no longer to be supported, are likely to over- throw the happiness of innumerable families; and the unavoidable impending revolution in the exis- ting relation of money, is likely to cause the ruin of thousands, who neglecting its virtual possession confided their welfare in its symbolic value. All this must happen, before the proud queen of the world will have learnt, to adopt herself to her new

situation, and to limit her necessities of nourishment, clothing and domestic regulations, to those
means of satisfying them, which her own soil offers.
Thus then, supposing, even that wisdom united with
energy guide the helm, the approaching future period is still likely to be so pregnant in tumultuous
agitations, and to carry along with it, so many privations, sufferings and misfortunes, as more than
amply to merit the just appellation of distressful
times, and the feeling mind cannot refrain from
casting an eye of commiseration upon the approaching generation, over whom such calamities impend.

If on the other hand, we do not estimate the
value of individual life, according to its feelings,
but its actions, and consequently judge of the passing existence of one generation, agreable to what
it contributes towards the attainment of the sublimest aim of human nature, the above picture would
turn out far more consolatory. For as this aim
towards which the lives of countless generations in-
cessantly incline, can be no other, than to represent reason on earth, and to tame the impetuous
passions within us, and the wilder powers of nature
without us, by means of voluntary laws, and so to
arrange the whole in harmony complete, that the
spirit, which is from God shall be predominant;
it is probable, that however cloudy the present per-
turbation may appear, the new form of things,

engendered from it, will still shew, that we have made
considerable approaches towards this most sublime
end. For brutal and arbitrary power, has undeniably been obliged to cede much ground, to those
exertions evinced every where, and made for the
attainment of a reasonable state of unanimity, either
by the governments in their frequent discussions on
the common affairs of our quarter of the globe, or
by the people, in their reigning tendency towards
a legal definition of the rights and privileges of
each order in the state. Struggles of this nature
cannot remain unfruitful, and the changes which
await commerce and the various branches of industry, will contribute most powerfully to their future
prosperity. The servitude and slavish dependence,
in which the acquirement of their daily bread, and
the struggle after physical existence, have hitherto
chained the majority of the mass of people will become less frequent; for in consequence of the blow,
the manufacturing system, extended beyond all
bounds, must necessarily suffer, the younger generation will be driven from the squallid habitations
of misery and infection, will spead itself over a more
ample surface of the earth, and will direct its activity to other employments of the mind. By this,
the decrease of competition in the ancient trades,
would ensure those who had remained to prosecute

(20)

them, a better price for their labour, and with it a more easy and unconcerned existence. Finally the more active participation in the affairs of the state, which must gradually fall to the share of the higher orders of the citizens, will raise in them, that respect for themselves, and that shame for the opinion of others, in which the seed of all civic virtue is contained; for the more uncontrouled and public, man lives under the influence of the law, the more disgust he internally feels for what is unworthy, but the more basely he be oppressed, the more vile will he become in his private actions. In one word, the energies of almost every individual have been awakened and from every side excited, by the distress of an age dreadfully calamitous; the misfortunes, which the abuse of these powers, and the savage raging of unbridled passions can bring upon mankind, stands in universal fresh and bloody remembrance *); on which account we ought not to disregard the warning lessons, and advice of the noblest among the people,

---

*) Humanity must shudder at the sanguinary acts committed lately at Palermo, but which afford another proof of the justice of the above remarks of the author, who no doubt alludes to the French revolution.

Translator,

who have pointed out those roads, which still present an opportunity of escaping from the labyrinth.
If the electrical shock, which, given in the West,
aroused Europe from her lethargy, has hitherto
operated almost universally in a destructive manner,
as the crude powers of nature are wont to do, it is
yet to be hoped, that the arts and sciences, in which
we shall still long remain predominant, will now
be able to accomplish in cool contemplation, their
work, of bringing to light from amidst the fermenting elements, the qualities of a noble and dignified human existence! —

XIII.

Returning to the point from which we started, and
placing before us the picture of America, as she offers
herself at present to the observer, and will likely be
developed in the future, the most perfect contrast
with the state of Europe fetters at once our attention. If the institutions in Europe be antiquated,
and an universal struggling be evinced, to overturn

the existing order of things, and to erect a new edifice upon the ancient base, the age of political wisdom in America, is on the other hand directed to the desirable aim, of allowing what is new and scarcely founded, to take root, and forming a national unison, common customs and a friendly affinity, by the force of habit. — In the first place we treat of the United States in the Northern hemisphere. That which here strikes the traveller and the European emigrant, as most remarkable, is according to their united testimonies, the division of interests the want of tranquillity of mind and native feelings, every one pursuing but his own views, and even forsaking with indifference the soil, that nourished him, if the hope of superior gain allures him into the newer Western lands on the Ohio and Missisippi; in one word, the more material feeling for, and exclusive attention to the acquirement of worldly wealth, which begets a restless and unsteady course of life, continually fed by new speculations, is predominant here, so that we may with justice assert, that the European will for a considerable time retain the ascendancy in the intellectual regions.

And still — what are we to expect otherwise in a state, which scarcely forty years independent, has witnessed only its second generation of free natives, and in conjunction with the original stock of British colonists, contains, on an immense surface, a thinly strewed population, composed of every European nation: Germans, French, Dutch, Swiss and Italians, who have neither language, descent, nor religion common with each other; the pursuit, after an actual maintenance, and the subsequent acquirement of wealth derived either from the soil, or mechanical ingenuity, alone congenial to them all, tends rather to disperse, than to combine them, in cordial proximity. The form of government contributes also to delay the fusion of the heterogeneous elements; for the former colonies aiming at the greatest possible freedom, were transformed into united states, each independent of the other, and only invested the common government of the whole, with so much of the power of sovereignty, as was just necessary, to present externally, the view of one political body, and to prevent internally, discord and civil war, as well as those obstacles, which one state might oppose, by means of prohibitory measures to another, and thus hinder the developement of the resources and industry of the whole. For this reason, the union is by no means a trunk grown from one common root, but an aggregate of foreign masses, which no natural bias, but universal law has united, to which, in the possession of freedom they have subjected themselves, in order, under its protection, to attain a state of prosperity.

In order to elevate themselves to this prosperity, or rather, only to insure themselves the means
of attaining it, — for as for enjoyment itself, the
majority have hitherto no time — no quicker resource presents itself, than that of commerce; hence
the mercantile spirit, which certainly is predominant in America, where even that which is most
immoveable — the soil — forms one of the most
important articles of trade. This spirit, every one.
breathes throughout his own peculiar profession;
and and instead of delivering the produce of his
industry upon order, to fixed customers, or contracting with the regular merchant for it, offers it for
sale in his own warehouse, or exports it on his
own risk, if his affairs are carried on upon a larger
scale. This propensity keeps the isolating and unsociable inclinations of men, as envy, avarice and
mean interestedness, in continual agitation, stifling
the birth of all sympathetic feelings, and preventing that exchange of ideas, which can never be called to light there, where the one would rather be
employed in anxiously watching the other, in order
surreptitiously to gain some advantage from his
neighbour. From this source undoubtedly flow that
coldness and unamiableness, and want of confiden-
tial effusions, which are prejudicial to sociableness
on the other side of the ocean; not less flows from
it, that estimation of the different branches of human

South Street in New York City, United States

Harvard College, Cambridge, Mass., United States

occupation, according to the net proceeds, they se-
verally return; and hence the indifference shewn
to arts and sciences, which offer an enjoyment of
a sublimer nature, than is necessary to him who is
still wholly engaged in what is earthly-practical. It
is easy to conceive how this spirit will operate upon
the course of education, and the culture of the rising generations; those branches will be particularly fostered, which enable man to assist himself without foreign aid, and speedily to earn a subsistence,
as the precursor of independence, which naturally
creating influence, soon renders its possessor, of importance in the state. Thus strength, and pliant-
ness of body, a ready power of combination, perseverance and an indefatigable resolution, as qualifi-
cations, which prevent the mind from sinking in
sullen moroseness, under the strokes of fortune,
and rather spur it on to renewed activity, will be
held in high estimation; those branches of positive
knowledge, which are immediately practical, and
profitable in a material point of view, will be learnt
in preference. And such is actually the case in America, generally, (for a description of this kind can
never mean but to represent the greater masses) and
nature, who first requires men to be rooted to the
soil, before she allows them to cast a view into the
æthereal regions, has here also remained faithful to
her principles. In what way she will lead this

rising people further, and unfold in them, a new history of the world and of mankind, we can only hazard some conjectures, founded on comparative information derived from the annals of more ancient nations.

The same propensity which exists in the unbridled character of youth to range the remotest parts and to grasp at the whole world, is found also prevalent in new states, which long invariably for aggrandizement and conquest, if not enclosed by nature, as Swisserland, within narrow and prescribed limits. Aminated by this propensity, did the inconsiderable city on the Palatine hill, composed of various descriptions of people, soar on high, until she became the mistress of the world; hurried away by it, did the Macedonian Alexander invade Asia, and grounded his monarchy, only dismembered so soon, by the premature death of its founder; instigated by it, did the unimportant kingdom of the Francs under Charles the Great, spread itself over Germany and Italy, as far as the Hispanian borders, and become adorned with the splendour of the renovated imperial diadem. The same impulse has extended the Russian territories, only become properly European in the last hundred years, to the gulph of Bothnia and the borders of Silesia in the West, and as far as the Black sea in the South. Neither has this inclination, as soon as the new state began to feel its strength, remained inert, in the North-American union, as may be amply seen by the acquisitions of Louisiana and the two Floridas, and its aggrandizement towards the Western Indian territories. During the last war, terminated by the peace of Ghent, the republic stretched its arms longfully towards Canada, and that this country still obeys the sceptre of Great Britain, may be principally attributed to a certain deficiency in military expertness and a want of determined measures. The disasters of this war, which have nevertheless not remained without compensative consequences, particularly, where the American navy had an opportunity of signalizing itself, have evidently brought more life and zeal into the preparatory dispositions, which are likely to ensure future success, and the more imposing the situation of the Union becomes, the earlier an ever-lurking jealousy is likely to afford her an opportunity, of trying her strength once more. Thus here, as formerly in the old world, war is likely to be the means of bringing those ingredients of this new people, which are yet foreign to each other, more rapidly into contact, of dissolving them into perfect harmony, of awakening national feelings, and of keeping more stedfastly alive, that enthusiasm for the good of the whole, which since the revolution appeared to have

(30.)

become dormant, but again burst forth, on the useless destruction of the Capitol by the British, and on
the attacks made by their squadrons on the defence-
less coasts. But if such a public spirit for the
grand interests of the nation, has once taken root,
and in the course of time beoomes diverted from political and external objects, to those of internal welfare, there is no result, however noble in its kind,
which this state may not flatter itself, with being
capable of bringing to light. The commercial spirit, engendered in the Atlantic, will find a powerful counterpoise in the greater stability of the truly
agricultural Western states, and, as agreable to our
premises, the more unnecessary, the commercial
intercourse with Europe becomes and which once
will finally cease, the more the communication of
the former states will encrease with the interior of
the vast continent, and will there, as well as in the
West India islands, be richly compensated for the
stagnated sale of those productions, which Europe
heretofore paid for, with the produce of her manufacturing industry. But the more the political bond,
torn asunder from all foreign relations, gains in
strength, and the internal intercourse becomes animated, the more, will the language, manners and
inclinations of the people assimulate themselves.
An American character and an American dialect
will arise. The English, as the language of the law

and the courts of justice, will it is true, ever form
the foundation of the latter, but through the intimate connexion with the several aboriginal as well
as emigrant people, so many foreign words will be
admitted, and from an incessant original developement of the mind, whose radiant beams language
represents, so many peculiarities will attach themselves to it, that in the lapse of a few generations,
not alone a national idiom, but even a particular
book-language is likely to spring up, to understand
which, the old English, will by no means be adequate. With this language, a peculiar code of erudition will also form itself, very dissimular possibly
to the present European one. Not the histories of
Greece and Rome, nor the languages of these states,
are likely, in future times to form the general basis
of scientific education; the study of the national history, from the time of the very first settlements,
and the language of the mother countries, from
which the descendants of the emigrants had derived
their extraction, would much more probably constitute its ground-work; and the investigation of
the origin, and gradual propagation of the primitive
inhabitants of the new world and of their languages
and monuments, is also very liable to shade in oblivion, not alone the Egyptian, Phoenician and Oriental, but even in the course of time, the Grecian and
Roman antiquities. But above all, the exploration

of the native soil, may be looked upon as the pri-
mary object of learned research, containing as it
certainly does, in the bosom of the mountains, in
the obscurity of the trackless forests, and on the immense plains, which have never felt the ploughshare,
nor scarcely the step of a lonely wanderer, an
abundant store of hitherto undiscovered treasures,
either belonging to the history of the antideluvian
world, or capable of benefiting future generations.
The practical propensity of this people, will probably combine with this research, an unremitting
study of mathematics, as well as of the chymical,
technical and oeconomical sciences, in order justly
to appreciate, and to make a true appropriation of
the above treasures. On the other hand, metaphy-
sics, and mere abstract efforts of the mind, are not
likely to gain ground for some time to come, appearing principally to flourish there, where a distinct learned order in the state exists, which in some
measure may be considered as a luxury and appen-
dage of a civil-society, long since sated and soaring
above any interest, physical life can ever afford,
and consequently incompatible with the necessities
of a nation, only first engaged in attaching itself to
the soil. No visible efforts can be expected in the
culture of taste or attention to the fine arts, until
the enthusiasm for one common country, and the
impression of nature, so inexhaustibly rich in the

sublimest scenes, as well as in calmer beauties and manifold charms, shall have fired some original ge_nius, to make her the theme of his immortal song, and the nation, in a state of greater composure, having laid aside their most pressing interests, shall possess a sense of feeling, sufficiently exalted, to estimate such works *). In the first place the

---

*) The striking picture, which Kant draws of an age, which contains the requisites for the discovery of a scale to regulate taste, and with it, a model for every fine art, would lead us to expect the appearance of such an epocha in America. We take the liberty of quoting it here, [as a favorable omen, observing only, that at the time it was drawn, (1790) the state of things was not then sufficiently developed in the new world, to have warranted this great man, in applying his ideas to the future state of that portion of the globe. —

"The preparatory study of all the fine arts, "if they are to be brought to their highest "degree of perfection, appears not alone to "lay in any given directions, but in the cul-"tivation of those intellectual qualities, by "means of those elementary principles, which "are called "h u m a n o r i a": probably because "humanity signifies on the one side, the ge-"neral feeling of participation, and on the

proficiency in oratory, which the public character
and the discussions of the legislative senates have

"other, the power of an intimate and uni-
"versal communication; which properties com-
"bined, constitute a state of happiness, suit-
"able to humankind, being thereby distin-
"guished from the limited faculties of the
"brute creation. That age as well as
"people, in which the active propensity
"evinced itself, of forming a social compact,
"which transforms a nation into a lasting
"community, and which impulse had to con-
"tend with the considerable difficulties, that
"embrace the weighty problem of uniting
"freedom, consequently equality, with
"constraint (more from veneration and
"submission to laws voluntarily enacted, than
"from a sense of fear): it would be necessa-
"ry for such an age and such a people first
"to invent the art of a reciprocal communi-
"cation of ideas, between the most polished
"and the most unrefined portion of the na-
"tion; to pay attention to the several grada-
"tions, which exist between the enlightened
"and cultivated state of the former, and the
"natural simplicity and originality of the
"latter; and thus to discover the medium
"between the highest possible cul-
"tivation, and man in a contented

rendered peculiarly the province of the American, is likely to emerge from that profusion of declamatory phraseology, which at present generally stamps it, and to exalt itself to that brilliant art, we admire in the legacies of a Demosthenes and a Cicero. May, it then, only subservient to truth and justice, never allow itself to be abused as a tool of factions, and in recommendation of pernicious measures!

"state of nature, which alone con-
"stitutes the true scale for taste,
"as an inherent human feeling, not
"to be governed by any general
"rules.

"A more advanced age will hardly
"render this model superfluous, as
"it will be continually departing
"more and more from nature, and
"not being in possession of any of
"her extant impressions, will at
"last be incapable of forming an
"idea of the happy union, in one and
"the same people, of the legal con-
"straint of the highest culture,
"with the power and correctness of
"nature, uncontrouled and sensible
"of her own dignity." —

It is reserved perhaps for America at some future time, to realize this idea.

For unfortunately, that incurable evil of the republics of ancient and modern times, political party-spirit, has not remained foreign to America; by this we by no means wish to designate a wise, and even vigorous opposition under the ægis of a sacred invulnerable existing constitution, but a passion for innovation directed against the forms and the actual organized institutions of the state   It is known, what concussions, the diverging tendency of the federalists and the anti-federalists has occasioned since the origin of the union; the latter are accused of wishing to slacken its bond, and to encrease the rights of the individual states, which would render the constitution more d e m o c r a t i c; whereas the former, are said to have only joined the present union, as being the most desirable thing for the moment, but to wish in their hearts, the executive power of the government encreased at the expence of the independence of the different States, and to evince an inclination for m o n a r c h i a l principles. — Even at present the greater part of the citizens, participating in the administration of affairs are divided into these parties, or are at least, as is ever the case, where party-spirit exists, looked upon as belonging to them. — Circumstances seem for the moment to give the federalists, or at least those of their party, who wish to have the power of the United-States-government upheld in its greatest extent, a considerable preponderancy. The danger threatened from England, to which the last war has more than ever turned the public attention, exacts, not less than the maintenance of the new acquisitions, the adoption of general measures, for fortifying the vulnerable points, encreasing the navy, and forming and strengthening the national army. But the execution ef such measures throughout the union, demands the employment of all the attributes of the executive power, consequently causes it to make its appearance oftner and in a stronger light. Other causes will gradually expand, which are apt to promote this tendency towards a more absolute form of government. — To these belong, the rapid encrease of the great trading cities in the Atlantic states, in which a mass of people disproportionate to the population of the internal country are crowded together, the wealth which accumulates there, the luxury and corruption of morals necessarily produced by it, the ebullition of the various passions, which, enclosed within narrow precincts, must light up a flame the more destructive and more difficult to be extinguished: all circumstances, which can awaken apprehensions for the undisturbed continuance of the present political - forms. What may prevent for a long time to come, the explosion of the

(31)

perturbed elements, and tend to secure the existing
state of things; is the necessity of unanimity for the
common defence in repelling the attacks, which
are to be apprehended from the conflict with the
jealousy of Europe, and the question of maritime superiority; as well as general want of a reciprocal
approximation, for the purposes of intercourse, as
soon as, according to the reasons we have laid down,
the communication with our quarter of the world
shall have ceased. But on America being once left
to herself, and fully secure from abroad, on her population having encreased in that proportion, which
is to be expected from the natural progress of culture and the incessant acquisition of emigrants,
and on a multitude of idle consumers on the one,
and of p a u p e r s out of employment on the other
side, having sprung up from this encrease; the epocha of turbulent popular commotions is then likely
to make its appearance, and the seed of discord to
shoot up; nearer interests and the isolation of the
powers, now less attractive or repulsive, by reason of
their greater scope for action, effectually stifle the
growth of this baneful plant at present. Then that
might easily happen, which on a surface of half the
globe, ought not to seem surprizing, of several c e n-
t r a l p o i n t s having formed themselves, each governing its sphere of attraction, and causing independent states to revolve around them; and if our

posterity should behold a royal throne raise itself
on the banks of the Potowmak, and a chair of Pre-
sidency over a Western federal - state situated on the
Ohio, that would only have occurred, which the
course of the world hitherto, most certainly autho-
rizes us to expect. For the principle of democracy
continues fermenting inwardly, and will strive to
shew itself somewhere, outwardly, and most naturally there, where the population given to agriculture, more than to the employments of the
citizen, only requires but a light rein, to curb the
overbearing disposition of natural freedom. —

There is still a tie, which originally was destined to check the savage mind, by the influence of
respect for invisible powers, and the hope and fear
derived from such, before the idea of a social compact organized agreable to equal laws, could gain
an ascendancy over it. We mean Religion,
which at first, adapted to the condition of its foster-
children, addressed itself only to the outward man,
in a sensual and as it were corporeal form, in order
to wean him from a state bordering on savageness,
to one of concord and morality, and to oppose the
barriers of social order to the eruptions of every
wild propensity. But on this care being entrusted
to the state, it had been the means of forming, it
addressed itself to the mind, in order to imprint on
it the harmony of virtue, which is subject to no law,
to plant in it the love, and the sacrifice of every

thing at the shrine of good, and to stamp it with that nobleness of feeling, which can render the descendant of heaven worthy of returning home, to the mansions of his eternal father. Then even, religion, as being a lasting institution for moral improvement, required a garb and outward form, about which, the understanding ever on the alert, soon differed, and which in order to be of stability, demanded the legal determination and the protection of the various states. Thus arose a church constitution, and with it, the dispute, never fully adjusted, regarding the relation in which, this church stands to the state. It is unnecessary to describe at large, how this contest was carried on in Europe, through the dark ages, or how the church remained triumphant, as long as the imagination and faith out of ignorance, or unsuspecting filial confidence, governed the nations, but how it was overthrown on the understanding having exerted its right of enquiry into the grounds of belief. Neither does it belong to our province to enter into, how a checkered mixture of sensual ceremonies and forbidden tenets, in those countries ruled by the sceptre of the church, upheld their obedience rather by the force of habit, but there, where liberty of conscience had been allowed, plainer forms called to light the more inward spiritual worth, and the doctrine began to be valued more than the rites, moral conduct more than outward ceremonies, and voluntary conscientious submission, more than the blind obedience of faith. — The American legislature has solved the problem of the precise relation of church to state, in a perfectly new way; having, in order to maintain the church belief, and to provide for a continual source for its propagation, made the adoption of the principal tenets of Christianity in some, and the decided profession of the doctrines of the Protestant church, in the most states, an exclusive condition, on which the rights of citizenship, and ability of being elected to public offices, and dignities, depended. — But the laws of the residue of the states, tolerate all religious opinions, and allow the Papists, who in the other states are particularly under restrictions, the full enjoyment of equal rights and privileges, but have left at the same time, the support of the church edifices, the endowment of the rites of worship, and the choice and maintenance of the ministry and other servants of the church, to the different congregations; and in order entirely, to prevent its interference in wordly matters, have by law excluded the clergy from all participation in the legislative and any other civil offices *),

---

*) According to the constitution of South Carolina, no one is capable of being an elector, who does

This organization of the ecclesiastical order, is in reality yet too new, and the condition of America has hitherto been too unsettled, to be able to form a judgment as to the probability of its duration; but a view taken of the human character

---

not profess the main doctrines of the Christian reli_gion; according to the laws of Massachussets, Delaware, Maryland, and North Carolina the profession of the Christian religion is sufficient; but according to those of New-Hamshire, Vermont, New-Jersey, South Carolina and Georgia, the belief in the Protestant religion expressly, constitutes eligibility to the legislative assemblies, and other public employments. The constitutions of Massachussets and Maryland, authorize the imposition of commune or district taxes, for the maintenance of the Protestant clergy, in the other states, the care of the ministry, is entirely left to the arbitrary will of their congregations. In New-York, Delaware and North Carolina, the clergy, are excluded by the letter of the constitution, from all public employments, in the other states, the same rule is almost generally, but only observed through the force of custom and habit. Agreable to the constitution of the Union, Congress can never make a law, which declares any particular religion to be the ruling one, or forbids the free exercise of any other.

would not acknowledge it to be compatible with the sublimer ends of religion, and consequently would seem to forebode a change taking place in it, sooner or later. As the possession of free landed property is esteemed the most honorable means of subsistence, being the most independent, so is the dignity of the human condition imparied, the further it removes itself from this state of freedom. — The servant in the pay of the state stands in this valuation below the land-owner, who receives from no one, and supports many; and again, far below him stands the private servant, let him have been hired by many or a single individual, for the performance of any particular business. But now it appears evident, that the ecclesiastic, in the sphere of the hired servile relation, into which he is undoubtedly banished in America, does not stand on his right place; for being the mediator between the law and personal caprice, he shall, by instruction and council, and a discharge of holy functions, exercise a superiority over the minds of his congregation, with which, the dependence on the good will and generosity of the members of his community, stands in as great a contrast, as the exercise of paternal authority does, with the provision made for the person of the father, by charitable donations of the children. Perhaps in America, and in all places, where the nature of the case is the same, it has not been

duly taken into consideration, that right alone ensures respect, and that the authority, whose subsistence depends on the caprice of those placed under
its sphere of action, stands at variance with itself.
— Therefore wiser predecessors, with a laudable
forethought, in those states, in which the church
being grown up together with the forms of the civil institutions, must necessarily exercise a greater
influence, have taken care, to secure its servants a
provision founded upon fixed rights, having assigned them either landed property, or suitable perpe-
tual dotations, not alone for their own support, but
that they might exercise the duties of benevolence,
and shew themselves as the fathers of the poor, to
whom the surplus of their income lawfully . belongs *). The correctness of this maxim loses

----

*) "Bona ecclesiæ non sunt episcoporum, sed paupe-
"rum, quorum procurationem quodammodo ge-
"runt. — Si pauperum compauperes sumus, et nos-
"tra sunt et illorum; si autem privatim, quæ no-
"bis sufficiant, possidemus, non sunt illa nostra,
"sed pauperum, quorum procurationem quodam-
"modo gerimus: non proprietatem nobis usurpa-
"tione damnabili vindicamus". These words borrowed from the letters of Saint Augustin, have at
all times formed the acknowledged principles of
the church.

nothing, in having been exaggerated by the superstition and weakness of bigoted souls, by priests
having abused these gifts for the purposes of ambition and an inordinate luxurious life, and by proud
bishops having revelled in superfluity, whilst the
lower orders of the clergy, standing in the nearest
connexion to the people, and working most for the
cause of religion, languished in want. The Luthe-
ran church reformation has put a barrier to the
above excess of wealth and political influence, and
those states which have remained firm to the old
church, have at least in this, faithfully followed the
example by partial reforms. — But the foundation
of a suitable maintenance for the clergy, out of
their own means, or rather from property lawfully
belonging to the church perpetually, (and not by
collections nor by a salary, bargained for at the ac-
cession of every new minister) has still been adhered to, and it is really to be wished, that the other
methods of supplying the deficiencies of too scanty
benefices, which have been introduced or retained,
by the side of the above foundation, might once be
again abolished. — The preacher of the word of
truth, ought not to receive even a part of his indispensible maintenance, as an immediate gift of
the children within his fold; it ought to be secured
to him, according to the ideas of justice, even

without the donations of the latter; but let the
community retain the desirable privilege, of sweet-
ening the life of their d i g n i f i e d minister, as
they would that of a beloved father, by marks of
attachment, and grateful esteem. Should America
ca once elevate herself to that state, which renders
the mind generally, more free from earthly cares,
and more susceptible for the sublimer intellectual
world, she will also see the necessity, of clothing
that order with more independence, whose duty it
is, to make the support of the spiritual feelings and
the improvement of the inward man, the only objects of its care; and by investing it with a greater
degree of external respect and more settled rights, it
will be stimulated to more benevolent activity. We
doubt not, that in the progressive ¦developement of
time, this rising people though at present sublu-
nary in their reflections, yet active and aspiring, will
arrive at the foregoing state; and then, that cordiality
and union of minds, that we have regretted the want of
at present, and which of individuals form a people,
of a people a community, being the visible emblem
of an invisible divine kingdom, will not fail to
make their bright appearance.

North America has hitherto no N o b i l i t y,
as little as she has an ecclesiastical order, and is too
young yet, as an independent body, to be able to
boast of ancient families. In the mean time, no

law will be able to prevent noble races from start-
ing up, and the tendency of honouring the merits
of celebrated ancestors, in the persons of their posterity, will operate as strongly here as in the old
world. A large landed estate, held in the hands of
one family, through many generations, forms of
itself, a species of patronage over the lesser inhabitants, who are dependent upon such possession, in
their traffic and modes of livelihood, and the administration of high state charges in the legislature or
the senates, honorably conducted by many of the
same name, ensures a celebrity, which considerably
assists the heir of such a name, in his secure entrance
into the world and his admission to a sphere of
greater activity, as it spares him the first and greatest exertion, of forcing himself into notice, from
amidst the obscure multitude. Such a nobility
America will also once possess, and it would still be
the happiest cast of the die, if she could confine
herself to this, which a renewed series of merits,
must constantly uphold and support. Nevertheless,
it may not be contradictory to admit, that an aristo-
cratical principle might even unfold itself in her
constitutions, as these in the course of time begin
to incline to the forms of monarchy, and that also
here, an order represented by birth might once
become necessary, for the purpose of forming a
durable barrier, against the extremes of human

errors: despotism, which subjects all to one common oppression, and the excess of democracy, which dissolves every thing in wild licentiousness. But whatever futurity may have in reserve for the riper ages of these states, they never can fail in attaining their high destination, as long as the fundamental pillars of their happy constitution, the equality of all in the eye of the law, and the publicity of their legislature as well as their tribunals, remain unimpaired.

From the states of the Northern Union, our view carries us to that immense territory, extending from the Western borders of Louisiana to the Pacific Ocean, and from thence across the isthmus of Darien to cape Horn, which has hitherto, with the exception of Brazil, done homage to the Spanish sceptre. It is difficult to determine, during the conflict for independence, in which large tracts of country are at present engaged, or even after having obtained their freedom, how the institutions of the new states are likely to form themselves; for what has hitherto, for the convenience of the organization of the insurrection, been constructed after the North-American model, may entirely be looked upon as provisional measures. For in this part of America, the road to the attainment of a new civil constitution, which would unite the state in security under equal laws, is by no means so even and

free from obstacles, as was the case in the North. On
the breaking out of the disturbances, there were not
here, as there, elements of a representative constitution; there were no assemblies for the discussion
of public affairs, and no fundamental law, which
secured the citizen against oppression. On the other
hand, the institutions of unlimited monarchy, the
pretensions of a religion the only one tolerated, and
even predominant in civil affairs, the power of a
nobility gifted with vast possessions, and the preju-
dices of the Whites, Mestizes, Mulattoes *), and Copper coloured natives, with their innumerable subdivisions, did, and still exist in great abundance.
And although South-America has undoubtedly a
considerable advantage over the United States, in
harbouring but an inconsiderable number of black
slaves within her bosom, whereas in North-America, they constitute nearly a seventh part of the whole
population **), yet the consequences are not to be

---

*) These three principal castes, the Spaniard classes
   under the common appellation of reasonable
   people (gente de razon) thereby lowering the
   Indians as it were, to the condition of brutes.

**) Essai politique sur le royaume de la nouvelle
    Espagne par Humboldt; à Paris 1811. 5 Vol. 8vo
    Tom. 1. pag. 221.

foreseen, which are liable to be produced, by the native Indians who are free, it is true, in the eye of the laws, but who have been for centuries oppressed by subordinate tyranny, and infamously robbed of their nobleness of character, awakening from their lethargy, as soon as the universal struggle after a better existence, and the gift of a more enlightened culture, dangerous in the beginning, shall have also reached them. For it cannot be denied, that it is no easy task, equitably to determine the future place which about two millions of aboriginal Mexicans shall take in society, or by the means which civilization offers, to put a stop to the inroads and depredations of the well-mounted Cumanches in New-Biscay, or the Patagonians near the straits of Magellan, or to reconcile the brave Araukanians to the new order of things. The existence of large and populous cities *), furnished with every art and all the refinements of luxury, and scarcely excelled by those of Europe, in corruption and depravity, is likely to exert a considerable influence on the organization of future forms of government, and on the course of the passing events.

---

*) Mexico 112,000, Lima 55,000, Buenos Ayres 40,000, Cusco 30,000, Montevideo 10,000 inhabitants &c. &c.

The tendency of such cities, is ever monarchial, and when revolutions begin, under such a political and moral state of things, which changed the constitution of the ancient Romans into an absolute monarchy, there is at least strong reason to believe that similar causes may produce like effects. And in the present case, it is of no inconsiderable weight, that the monarchial government, which has now for more than twelve years been indigenous in Brazil, will rather favor those of the insurgent Spanish provinces, whose wishes incline to similar forms; for on republican constitutions being universally introduced, it could hardly hope to maintain its own existence, against the inward fermentations of discontented minds, or the outward pressure of neighbouring republics. — Neither is it to be expected, that one and the same form of government will be found adapted to every part of such an immense territory; there, where a numerous population be crowded together in a disproportionate narrow compass, a central power may rather appear most fit; whereas in less populated districts of greater extent but looser connexion, local, or Canton constitutions, and a federal-tie, rather embracing the whole, than fitting closely, may be considered most appropriate. — The Southern half of America is likely to become much sooner independent of Europe in a commercial respect, than the Northern part, for it will receive its succours, from the latter, and will pay for these with those precious metals which hitherto flowed to Europe. Thus an internal and coasting trade will be opened between the two preninsulas, rendering them entirely independent of the rest of the world, which will only then present itself, as an object subservient to their future possible plans of aggrandizement.

The internal affairs of South America are not likely to be so soon settled. For although the less numerous tribes of Indians in the Northern hemisphere, continually forced farther back by the increase of settlers, and enervated by the immoderate use of spirituous liquors, must gradually become extinct; the hardy and numerous nations in the South, may possible find means nevertheless of maintaining themselves; and the spectacle may be reserved for posterity, of viewing the gradual progress of these nations from the lowest steps of cultivation, to the highest point of civilization, and of beholding independent states of American indigenous people, entering into the ranks of kingdoms, founded by the descendants of European emigrants. It can only be the lot of future centuries to ascertain, what shape religion will assume amongst them, what forms of government and civil institutions will develope themselves, and how the mixture of European culture and Indian originality will operate upon the whole. But according to all probability, the Southern part of America being richer and more vigorously endowed by nature, is likely also to exhibit more interesting results for the history of the human race, than North America, whose people in their further developement, are more apt again to approach the model of their transmarine ancestors, than to unfold a new picture of life formed of original elements. —

XIV.

We have yet to take a view of the other portions of the globe, which are only at present of importance, in as far as they are subservient to the purposes of Europe and America, but not from any active link they form in the chain of civilization. We have already noticed, that the coasts of the Mediterranean, in Africa and Asia, are likely to return under European dominion and protection and that Greece will reflourish under new forms, as soon as limits be put to the pernicious nuisance of Turkish sovereignty. Persia, whose civilization has only

been hindered by the want of a settled form of government, and the unhappy wars of succession, which
have invariably been the consequence of Oriental
politics, perfectly undetermined on this head, may
possibly even sooner, enter into the line of cultivated nations, on account of her intimate connexion
with Russia. The reception of a resident Russian
embassy, contrary to all the former usages of Asiatic governments, has made a great step towards this
aim. The bible-societies have also found an entrance there, and in conjunction with the religious
main object, the encouragement to learn those
languages, which have not been admitted within
the literary sphere, as preparatory to a nearer
intercourse with those nations hitherto without
the limits of modern civilization, is possibly not
one of the smallest collateral causes of the zeal,
with which the British nation supports these societies. No person of information will deny, that Persia, unanimous in herself and relying upon Russia,
may one day become dangerous to the British dominion in the East Indies, under the cooperation of
the independent and discontented nations to the
North, and North-West of the territories of the
English company; nor can it be doubted, that the
native Indians as well as the rival European powers
would rather behold this extensive kingdom under
a native government, than under the present mer-

●antile administration on the other side of the Ocean.
Enclosed within Asiatic Russia to the North, and
Persia, the East Indies and China to the South, are
those numerous races of people, who in the thir-
teenth and fourteenth centuries, came forward as
conquerors of the world, and of whose dominion,
since the overthrow of the Indian Mogul empire,
there is no monument left, but in the reigning
Chinese dynasty, descended from the Tartar conquerors. These vast territories undoubtedly contain a
nursery of hardy and enterprising nations, from
which a new Ghingis-chan could once emerge, to
rouse the people of China from their lethargy, and
to awaken those energies, which, by the influence of
the same customs for a thousand years, have become
benumbed and stupefied, rendering every conception of new ideas, or approach towards renovated
forms, physically impossible. Reports of commotions in this vast kingdom, not entirely rejectable,
and renewed from time to time, have reached us;
and the impossibility, which Europe may soon find
herself placed in, of continuing her trade thither
in the usual manner by sea, will most assuredly contribute, to the commercial communication, which
has already been opened, from Kjachta on the confines of Tartary, through Siberia towards Moscow,
being more frequently made use of by caravans in
the Asiatic manner. By this very road then, it is

possible, (trade being invariably the precursor of a higher state of civilization) that new ideas and the various European sciences, may flow back to those countries, and which may be the means of bringing forth a better organization of their religious and civil institutions. — Thus changes are gradually preparing themselves in these extensive countries, which are likely to lead their inhabitants, from a life of mere sensual enjoyment, and an activity only directed to the purposes of animal existence and the savage impulse of violence, to intellectual necessities and exertions, and will unfold in them, the sublimer ends of human nature. — Most assuredly it would be a grand idea, were Europe, who is indebted to Asia, for her primitive knowledge, her culture of the human mind and her religions, immediate gifts, as it were, from the divine hand, destined to restore her, these presents perfeated by meditation, and matured by the labours of thousands of years.

The future fate of Africa lies veiled in deeper obscurity We are only acquainted with the coasts of this land of wonders, and have but a very scanty knowledge of its interior from the Mediterranean to the 12th or at the most the 11th degree of Northern latitude, and from its Southern extremity, scarcely beyond the 30th degree upwards. Those prodigies, nature may conceal within its bosom, will only be revealed to the investigators of future times, on having more successfully followed up the traces of those heroes of discovery, who not alone staked but sacrificed their lives, to a thirst of enquiry so beneficial to mankind. But the great enigma is, and remains, the appearance of mankind in a race, whose color, hair and other characteristic signs, intimate a most ancient consistency and a line of generations produced on the same soil, and unmixed since the lapse of the remotest ages, without having risen any - where, as far as our own, and the knowledge gained from caravans from the most distant quarters reach, above the first steps of intellectual developement. The opinion was therefore entertained formerly, that the actual negro race, was a variety in the human species, superior indeed in corporeal flexibility, and sensual qualities and acquirements, but far inferior in natural capacity of mind to the original race of Caucasus, and that in order that no link should be wanting in the chain of beings, it occupied the medium between the intellectual man, and the most perfect ape. Later experience, and the enquiries of physiologists into the construction of the negro, have, it is true, in individual instances completely refuted the above opinion; but at the same time it is not impossible, that the interior of Africa might present us with the picture of a primeval world, actually in being, in

which the existence of the forefathers of the present
human generation, at first only vegetative and then
awakened to animal sensuality, passed away without
a trace. At least, as the history of the human race,
as far as we are acquainted with it, strictly follows
in its progress, the developement of individual life,
from adolescence to the maturity of manhood, it
may undoubtedly be allowed to presume, that an
earlier state, corresponding with that of infancy,
which is unconscious of its being, may have prece-
ded that period, in which, perhaps after an obscure
existence of many ages, a holy tradition takes up
the history of man, then come to a knowledge of
himself, and awakened to a sense of good and evil.
But no one, who is acquainted from the course of
history, with the gradual developement of civilization, which only advances from land to land at isolated distances, never being discovered every where
at one and the same time, can find it contradictory,
that it is possible we may yet behold a model of the
foregoing state of mankind, still on earth. What
we learn from observation, of the negro-nations
hitherto known to us in the interior, places them
at the point of an existence purely sensual, given
to every impulse of animality, possessed of just so
much understanding and dexterity, as are requisite
for satisfying their necessities, or rather of preparing nature for the purposes of an instinct of im-

provement already awakened in them, but still ignorant of the force of reason and the dictates of conscience. For the negro is ingenious, and disposed to all kinds of work, carelessly chearful as a toyish boy, obedient, when well used, but also revengeful, savage and ferocious in his passions, as the tiger of his deserts, when irritated, and cold, without remorse and tears, on having accomplished any act of violence; at the same time prone to theft, without an idea of the sanctity of property, like the child, who without hesitation appropriates every thing to itself, it sees before it. Time will shew, if races may not be discovered, approaching nearer to the original state of childhood, than these people, who have arrived at the degree of man, in a complete sensual condition. Those who are already known, and particularly the inhabitants of the coasts, will be liable to greater advances, by their coming more frequently in contact with the civilized world; and were the abolition of the slave-trade to succeed, not alone in laudable resolutions, but in reality, and were the lawless subjection of the negroes, transformed into an obedience under paternal guardianship, a stain which disgraces humanity, would be wiped away, and the education of these children of nature, would no longer as hitherto, be purchased by blood and nameless cruelties. — The indefatigable endeavours of the British African society, and the closer connection, which Africa will come into with rising America, warrant us to expect a most favorable result in this respect; and on this ground, a more solid hope is to be erected, than on the duration of the new negro-kingdom in Haiti, which appears to be but at present an incongruous essay, which, the measure of the intellectual faculties of both rulers and people, is very possibly insufficient, to bring to a prosperous consistency.

From the abominations, with which this attempt has defiled the leaves of modern history, the eye turns with satisfaction to yon blooming colony in New South Wales, which founded by the refuse of European malefactors, has in less than thirty years *), by the adoption of rigid but wise measures combined with those of forbearing humanity, grown to a population of upwards of 25,000 souls, who are not alone in possession of every necessity of life, but have different articles for exportation, which they give in exchange for those conveniences of civilized life, that are familiar to the main stock

---

*) The first settlement in Botany Bay took place in the year 1787. "Watkin Tench's narrative of the expedition to Botany Bay with an account of New South Wales, London 1789, contains full particulars of it.

of the inhabitants from the time of their residence in their mother country. If the discoveries in this island, exceeding Europe in size, be prosecuted in the degree they have commenced, and population and culture encrease in an equal ratio, a commercial depot will be also established here, which linked in the chain of the civilized world, will perhaps once unite the greater part of the islands dispersed in the Australian seas, under the wings of its protection.

Should the author have succeeded in having inspired a heart here and there, with a greater love for the cause of humanity, and in having held forth the sources of misery in a clearer light, for the benefit of those who wish to see, and have the power of acting; should a considerable or even a small part of what has been argued, conjectured, even perhaps only dreamt of in the foregoing work, stand the test of experience, — it will not have been without its advantages.

The reader is kindly requested to excuse the errors of the press, which have unavoidably crept into the present work, occasioned by the setter's total ignorance of the English language; the following are pointed out, as particularly prominent.

Page	Line			read	
V.	11.	for :	oetherial	read	æthereal
3.	7.	—	pirvatical	—	piratical
11.	13.	—	is	—	it
18.	12.	—	Thamse	—	Thames
32.	17.	—	sword a to	—	sword to
74.	(in the note)		James II	—	James IId's son
174.	16.	—	likeep	—	keep
191.	23.	—	not to sink	—	not sink

Postscript

In the twentieth century, and especially after the Second World War, when the dominance of the Soviet Union and the United States in world affairs has been so obvious, reference has often been made to Tocqueville's famous prophesy about the future greatness of the two big fringe powers, America and Russia[1]. This has been seen as the astonishing and inspired first forewarning to the people of Europe by a genius that their days as world rulers were numbered. It has only in recent years been realized, through Tocqueville studies and study of the ideas about America and Russia which were current in Europe in the eighteenth and nineteenth centuries, that Tocqueville's prediction if anything only set the seal on a long and intense debate on the future of America and Europe; in his prophesy, 'a lively discussion that had been going on for many years is re-echoed'.[2] Among the participants in this discussion we find the Danish official Schmidt-Phiseldeck with the present

---

De la démocratie en Amérique, I. (1835) (Conclusion): 'chacun d'eux i.e. America and Russia] semble appelé par un dessein secret de la Providence à tenir un jour dans ses mains les destinées de la moitié du monde'

BARRACLOUGH, G., 'Europa, Amerika und Russland in Vortellung und Denken des 19. Jahrhunderts' [Europe, America and Russia, in the Conception and Thinking of the 19th Century], *Historische Zeitschrift,* 203, 1966, 280–315, p 282.

260

work, in its time widely disseminated in Europe, which Tocqueville presumably knew, at any rate at second hand.[3] It is as, unquestionably, the principal Danish contribution to the literature on America in the nineteenth century, and as one of the central works of the Restauration period in this genre, that *Europe and America* is here reissued.

I. Life of Schmidt-Phiseldeck

Conrad Georg Friedrich Elias von Schmidt-Phiseldeck was born on 3 July 1770 at Brunswick in the then North German duchy of Wolfenbüttel, where at the time his father was a professor of constitutional law and history at the Collegium Carolinum. His mother, Marie Katharine Louise Crell, was a professor's daughter from nearby Helmstedt.

The boy grew up during the years when the American War of Independence (1775–1783) was agitating the public mind in Europe. Although concrete evidence is lacking, it is reasonable to suppose that the foundation of the grown man's interest in America was laid during his childhood. Nor is it impossible that he was brought into contact very early in his learned home with the results of the extensive American studies, centered on the university of Göttin-

[3] FABIAN, B., 'Alexis de Tocquevilles Amerikabild' [Alexis de Tocqueville's Picture of America], *Beihefte zum Jahrbuch für Amerikastudien*, I. Heidelberg, 1957, p 96.

gen, which flourished in North Germany in the last 25 years of the eighteenth century.[4]

After qualifying for university in 1787, Schmidt-Phiseldeck read theology and philosophy at the university of Helmstedt, at the same time cultivating his extensive literary interests.

Rather fortuitously, his path was directed a couple of years later toward Denmark through acquaintance with Constantin Brun, a Danish merchant highly regarded in political circles.[5] Schmidt-Phiseldeck became his son's tutor, and after travels in Switzerland, Germany and France with the Brun family arrived in Copenhagen, which he never again left except on official business. He never visited America, a fact which one of his more traveled critics would later point out.[6] He continued his studies in Copenhagen, taken the university examination in theology and philosophy and gaining a doctorate in philosophy (1791). After a time during which he was active

---

[4] SKARD, S., *American Studies in Europe*, I. Philadelphia, Penn., 1958, p 218.

[5] How the acquaintanceship came about is not clear. Possibly it was through Schmidt-Phiseldeck's father, who enjoyed a contemporary reputation as a considerable connoisseur of Russia. Constantin Brun, traveling to Russia for his government, may well have found it opportune to visit this man before negotiating with the Russians.

[6] 'Dr. Von Phiseldeck (nok Fiddlestick), who is not only a doctor of philosophy but a knight of Dannebrog to boot, has never been in America, but he has written a prophesy, showing that the United States must and will govern the whole world ...' TROLLOPE, F., *Domestic Manners of the Americans*. London, 1927 (1832), p 280.

as a philosophical author and public lecturer at the university, he began, now aged about 25, to apply himself to the political sciences. This he did with public aid and on the recommendation of the prime minister, Count Schimmelmann, a friend of the Brun family. In 1797, this man of all-round education, who had acquired Danish citizenship in 1794, entered the Danish central administration as an assessor in the *Generallandøkonomi- og Kommercekollegium* [department of agronomy and commerce].

In the difficult years during and after the Napoleonic Wars he was one of the most widely employed officials in the economic administration, and his star rose fast. In the years 1813–18, as director of the National Bank he occupied one of the country's most important administrative posts. Passage of the bank into private hands (1818) secured for him a few years' relief from his official duties. He was placed on an allowance and employed his time in writing his principal works, including this one. At his death in 1832 he was a deputy in the *Generaltoldkammer- og Kommercekollegium* [department of customs and commerce].[7]

II. Schmidt-Phiseldeck's authorship

Alongside his duties as a public official, Schmidt-Phiseldeck displayed throughout his life a voluminous

[7] Biographical material on Schmidt-Phiseldeck: *Allgemeine Deutsche Biographie*, XXIII. Leipzig, 1891; *Dansk Biografisk Leksikon*, XXI. Copenhagen, 1941 (with references), and ERSLEW, T. H., *Almindeligt Forfatter-Lexicon*, III. Copenhagen, 1853 (with references).

authorship which testifies to an astonishing capacity
for work as well as multifarious interests and wide
knowledge.[8] The philosophical activity of his youth,
which was strongly influenced by Immanuel Kant,
continued all through life, and a work of 1828, *Die
Welt als Automat und das Reich Gottes: Ein Beitrag zur
Religionsphilosophie* [The World as an Automaton and
the Realm of God; A Contribution to the Philosophy
of Religion], is regarded as his main philosophical
work. In the field of aesthetics, he published both
critical essays and original poems. A volume of translations of Modern Greek folk poetry[9] indicates his
extraordinary linguistic knowledge. At the same time, it bears attractive witness to the sympathy for the
Greek people which he shared with so many of his
contemporaries, and which in less attractive form
also comes out in *Europe and America* (chapter X). In
fact, his high regard for the Greeks was accompanied
by intense denigration of the Turks, whom he be-
lieved should be expelled from Europe.

In economics and politics we find Schmidt-Phiseldeck active in the most diverse spheres. He wrote

[8] Author's bibliography in ERSLEW, *op. cit.* From 1806
Schmidt-Phiseldeck was a member of the Danish Academy of
Sciences. Both as public servant and as author he won great recog-
nition for his achievements in his new country.
[9] *Auswahl Neugriechischer Volkspoesien, in deutsche Dichtungen umge-
bildet* [Selection of Modern Greek Folk Poetry, rendered into
German]. Brunswick, 1827.

about the status of Jews in Christian societies[10] and he
published papers on monetary theories, warmly ad-
vocating the metal standard; i.e., he regarded precious metals as the sole possible basis of a sound
monetary system.[11] These theories, which he was not
alone in holding at that time, had their background
in the monetary chaos of the previous decade, which
had badly hit Denmark. Today they have to be read
with great reserve. Similar reservations must of
course be made with regard to chapter XI of *Europe
and America,* where Schmidt-Phiseldeck describes the
consequences bound to arise in Europe as a result of
the reduced flow of gold from America to be expected after the independence of the western hemisphere. Schmidt-Phiseldeck was also active in the
more strictly journalistic field, both as a pamphleteer,
writing on his own and on the goverment's behalf,
and as co-editor over a long period of the official
commercial and industrial journal, *Handels- og Industri-Tidende* (1798–1810).

His outstanding achievement, however, as a politi-

[10] *Om den jødiske Nations hidtil værende Forhold til det christne Borger-
samfund, og dens Omdannelse i Fremtiden* [On the Jewish Nation's
Relation to Christian Society hitherto, and its Transformation in
the Future]. Copenhagen, 1817.
[11] The most important is: *Ueber den Begriff vom Gelde* [On the
Concept of Money]. Copenhagen, 1818. On Schmidt-Phiseldeck's
monetary theories: SVENDSEN, K. E., 'Dansk Pengehistorie
1700–1914' [Danish Monetary History, 1700–1914], in *Dansk Pengehistorie* [Danish Monetary History], I. Copenhagen, 1968, pp
120–21.

cal writer and as an author at all, must surely be the three books which he published in quick succession in the years 1820–22: *Europa und Amerika* (1820), the present work; *Der europäische Bund* (1821) [The European Union]; and *Die Politik nach den Grundsätzen der heiligen Allianz* (1822) [Politics according to the Principles of the Holy Alliance]. While his other writings are today scarcely remembered, these three books have assured him a lasting place in the literature. They were published in Copenhagen, but all were written in German: not that Schmidt-Phiseldeck could not write Danish, for in several aspects of his authorship he demonstrated that he could, but presumably because through his mother tongue he could communicate directly with a larger European readership. The books were published separately; but as Schmidt-Phiseldeck himself points out in the foreword to the book on the Holy Alliance, they belong together. It seems reasonable to regard them as a sort of trilogy, comprising the following parts:

(1) *Europe and America.* In the setting of a sketch of the course of world history since American independence (1776) the book gives a general assessment of future relations between the continents, especially Europe and America. The future of America is painted in glowing colours: this vast continent, which, unlike Europe, controls every conceivable natural wealth and raw material, holds all the potentialities. With the liberation of the United States, and the

independence of South America expected soon to follow it, they will now be fully realized. America will become the dominant continent, politically, economically and intellectually.

In contrast, the future of Europe is presented in sombre colours. Europe's power has to a wide extent been based, not on its own resources, but on the colonial system's exploitation of the resources of other continents, including free access to the riches of America. With the loss of America, however, the continent finds itself in a difficult situation, which may be expected to be aggravated by America's penetration as a major commercial power into Europe's other spheres of interest (Africa and Asia). Europe will lose its world dominion and hard times are impending for the old continent, with material distress and social misery.

Schmidt-Phiseldeck, however, believes that in the long term Europe has new possibilities, but only if it pays heed to contemporary demands and learns to depend on itself; if it cannot, then it must perish. Europe must turn to itself and its own potentialities, which have been neglected for colonial resources. It will have to abandon its internal political anarchy and unite under a common political system, and instead of applying its energies in overseas colonialism must regain its own territory by expelling the Turks from the countries of European civilization.

(2) *The European Union* takes a closer look at the problems of European union. As shown by the pre-

vious book, some such union would be necessary if Europe was to hold its own in the long run. The prior conditions and the possibilities of European union are discussed in the light of the common culture and fairly uniform political and social structure of the various states. Finally, there is a detailed discussion of how such an European union should be organized (defense system, form of government, currency, etc.).

(3) *Politics according to the Principles of the Holy Alliance.* In this work the author discusses the Holy Alliance in greater detail[12] as a connecting link between the yet utopian European federal state and the preconditions of such a future state, inherent in Europe's common cultural heritage, etc. For Schmidt-Phiseldeck, the Holy Alliance is proof that the European union so necessary no longer needs only to reach for 'the wide spaces of mere speculation', but can be based on something tangible.

This final part of the trilogy is the most dated in its approach and the least readable today. *The European Union,* which describes boldly and in detail how a European federal state should be organized, partly

[12] The Holy Alliance was signed by the Russian Czar, the Austrian Emperor and the King of Prussia on 26 Sept. 1815, and was joined subsequently by most other European countries. The document declared that 'the precepts of Justice, Christian Charity and Peace ... must have an immediate influence on the Councils of Princes and guide all their steps'. The Alliance is often identified, unjustly, with the reactionary policies of Russia, Prussia and Austria in 1815–1848.

on the pattern of North America, can still be read with profit and has assured Schmidt-Phiseldeck of a modest place among the many fathers of the European idea.[13] The greatest interest, however, attaches to the first part of the trilogy, the one here reproduced. It must be accounted one of the most absorbing of many attempts in the Restauration period to take the pulse of the time and indicate the lines of historical development as they appeared after the violent events of the preceding years and American independence a half-century earlier. It is with good reason that the work has been called 'prophetic';[14] though it should be said that Schmidt-Phiseldeck's wish was not only to foretell the future but also to influence and help to shape it. He wanted to confront the people of Europe with the contemporary realities, thereby opening their eyes to the conditions which had to be fulfilled in order to arrest Europe's decline.

[13] Vide *e.g.*, GOLLWITZER, H., *Europabild und Europagedanke* [Picture of Europe and Idea of Europe]. Munich, 1964 pp 197–200; MEULEN, J. ter, *Der Gedanke internationalen Organisation* [The Idea of International Organization], II, 1. The Hague, 1929, pp 185–93; BJØL, E., 'La Danimarca e l'Europa' [Denmark and Europe], *Rivista Danese,* special edition, 1971, pp 22–25.
[14] BAGGE, P., *Johan Nicolai Madvig. Et Mindeskrift* [Johan Nicolai Madvig: A Memorial Volume], I. Copenhagen , 1955, p 151.

III. The intellectual background to 'Europe and America'

There is no reason to suppose that Schmidt-Phisel-deck, any more than Alexis de Tocqueville (his junior by 35 years and far better known), got his ideas about America out of his own head. He was a well-read and industrious man, and it has also been said that he 'extracted much'.[15] Quite clearly, it must be assumed that he drew on the voluminous scholarly, polemical and political literature about America that grew up, so to speak, with him. In trying to unravel the sources to which he was particularly indebted when compiling *Europe and America*, however, we face a problem. His notes to the book are so limited that they cannot conceivably provide any realistic picture of his reading. Since, furthermore, we lack any information about the details of his intellectual development from any other source, a few simple indications of the European literature about America up to 1820 must take the place of a detailed account of the author's sources.

In *Europe and America* two great contemporary currents, as it were, converge: (1) the idea of America as 'the land of the future' (Hegel), and (2) the wide-

[15] MØLLER, J., 'Nekrolog. Conferentsraad v. Schmidt-Phisel-deck' [Obituary: Counsellor v. Schmidt-Phiseldeck], *Dansk Littera-tur-Tidende*, 1833, 261–70; 281–84, pp 268–69. Jens Møller knew Schmidt-Phiseldeck personally. On Tocqueville's sources: FABI-AN, B., *op. cit.*

spread pessimism of the post-Napoleonic period about the future of Europe. The concept of America as the land of the future has deep roots in seventeenth- and eighteenth-century Europe. America emerged very early as the country without the social injustice which characterized old Europe. America was the 'new Jerusalem'[16] that would become 'a better Republic than Plato's, and a grander Utopia than More's.'[17] Round these notions there gradually crystalized more many-faceted and more precise ideas about the nature of America's contemporary and especially future superiority. In particular, American independence in 1776 and the establishment of a democratic state strongly stimulated the conception of America as the land of the future in respect of political and social organization. America was 'the hope of mankind. It can become the model for it'.[18]

With the steadily growing economic and political importance of the United States, new aspects were soon added. Already from the 1770s the outlines of a new commercial, political and military giant were glimpsed; and from the turn of the century there was no longer any doubt. Whatever one might think of

[16] Expression by Samuel Sewall, cf. TYLER, M. C., A History of American Literature during the Colonial Time, II. New York/London, 1897, p 101.

[17] BERKELEY, G., An Essay towards preventing the Ruin of Great Britain. London, 1721.

[18] Turgot in a letter of 1778, cf. TURGOT, A. R. J., Oeuvres, ed. Gustave Schelle, V. Paris, 1923, p 539.

America, of its cultural level and of its political system (and on these opinions could differ), everybody agreed about the enormous wealth and potential of America. 'The phenomenal rise of American maritime commerce'[19] aroused concern, and there were vivid descriptions of the immense population growth that would multiply the number of America's inhabitants in the nineteenth century alone. 'The image of the energetic, growing adolescent' flowed 'inevitably' from the pen of every observer.[20]

To sum up, the fact had to be faced that 'these rebel colonists [United States] are in the process of becoming a strong and powerful people among the nations of the world. They are climbing with rapid strides toward the greatest of destinies'.[21] And was it not just the tip of the iceberg one saw? The potential of South America was rated very highly, and it was a widely held view, shared by Schmidt-Phiseldeck, that after its liberation South America would quickly surpass the United States. Compared with the United States, which seemingly was without any problems, and compared in the long view with the whole of the great American continent, Europe in the years toward the end of the Napoleonic era, and even more in the period thereafter, was seen in wide circles as an effete

---

[19] ECHEVERRIA, D., *Mirage in the West*. Princeton, 1957, p 236 (quotation from Turreau de Linières).
[20] *op. cit.,* p 240.
[21] *op. cit.,* p 241 (quotation from Hyde de Neuville). Numerous observations, variations on this theme can be found. See, *e.g.:*

bankrupt, overburdened with debt, encumbered with insoluble social problems. It was moreover economically dependent on a colonial system whose foundations, with the independence of the United States and the impending liberation of South America, were crumbling. Many of the reflections that were then made about America led almost inevitably to a comparison with Europe. And Europe must lose ground; that was appreciated everywhere, also in Denmark, which after the loss of Norway (1814) and violent economic convulsions, culminating in national 'bankruptcy' in 1813, was more affected by the defeatist mood than most countries. Against this background it was only natural in a work which sought in 1820 to balance the destinies of the two continents against each other, to forecast America's continuing ascendancy. All things considered, however, Schmidt-Phiseldeck's optimism with regard to Europe's future possibilities can seem astonishing.

ECHEVERRIA, D., *op. cit.;* ELOVSEN, H., *Amerika i svensk Littera-tur 1750–1820* [America in Swedish Literature, 1750–1820]. Lund, 1930; BARRACLOUGH, G., *op. cit.* How widespread these views were may be deduced from the attention paid to America in periodicals and newspapers all over Europe. In Denmark, for example, the *Handels- og Industri-Tidende* (which Schmidt-Phiseldeck edited for several years), carried numerous comments on America's rapid rise as an economic great power, while *Danske Statstidender,* from the middle of the second decade of the 19th century, printed the President's annual message to Congress.

IV. Schmidt-Phiseldeck's originality

In the light of the international literature current about 1820, which it may be assumed that Schmidt-Phiseldeck was largely familiar with, it can scarcely be claimed that he was in any essential respect original in his inferences about the relationship of America and Europe in the strict sense that he was 'the first' to think these ideas. Compared with the contemporary writers who discussed this relationship, it was not his merit that he prophesied America's future greatness, for he was by no means the one and only prophet. It was that, fairly briefly, clearly and concisely, in a simple and accessible work, he assembled and focused for discussion, as it were under a burning-glass, a synthesis of ideas that in the preceding decades had circulated in ever wider numbers in books, periodicals and newspapers. This assessment is true both in the perspective of history and in the contemporary view: the book was a great success, was translated into several languages, and was widely reviewed.[22]

V. The English translation and the translator

The translation was done in 1820, the year of the original publication, by Joseph Owen, an English-

[22] See *Bibliography of editions, translations and reviews*, p 275–77.

born manufacturer who had been living in Copenhagen from about 1813.[23]

The translation, which was a labor of love, elicited
great praise from its Danish reviewer,[24] who called it
'successful, easy and flowing', and, comparing it with
the original 'in some of the most difficult passages,'
thought it 'most perfectly' expressed the same, 'as
much as the different geniuses of the two languages
permitted it'. Whether the reviewer fully meant what
he wrote, or whether it was the pleasure of seeing a
Danish work, albeit written in German, translated
into a foreign language so quickly which inspired the
superlatives, must remain open. At any rate, it has to
be confessed that in several respects the translation of
Schmidt-Philseldeck's admittedly crabbed German
does not quite match up to modern standards of
translation, particularly as regards the demands of
exactitude.

[23]On Joseph Owen: *Dansk biografisk Leksikon*, XVII. Copenhagen,
1939, pp 527–28 (with references). On Owen's other literary work:
ERSLEW, T. H., *op. cit.*, II. Copenhagen, 1847.
[24] GIERLEW, A. C., in *Dansk Litteratur-Tidende*, 1820, pp 632–35.

Bibliography of editions, translations and reviews of 'Europe and America'

Editions

Europa und Amerika oder die künftigen Verhältnisse der civilisirten Welt. Copenhagen, 1820, X, 248 pp

Idem. Zweite Auflage mit Berichtigungen und Zusätzen. Copenhagen, 1820, XIV, 302 pp

Idem. Zweite Skizze [second version]. Copenhagen, 1832, VI, 286 pp

Translations

French: *L'Europe et l'Amérique, ou les rapports futurs du monde civilisé* par Mr. C. F. de Schmidt-Phiseldeck. Traduit de l'allemand par *** [= M. le comte Santi], Copenhagen MDCCCXX, XIV, 265 pp

English: *Europe and America or the relative state of the civilized world at a future period.* Translated from the German of Dr. C. F. von Schmidt-Phiseldek, by Joseph Owen. Copenhagen, 1820, [X] VIII, 257 pp

Danish: *Europa og Amerika eller den civiliserte Verdens fremtidige Forhold.* Af Dr. C. F. von Schmidt-Phiseldek. Oversat og forsynet med Anmærkninger af D. Didrichsen og H. A. Martensen. Copenhagen, 1820, XIV, 224 pp

Dutch: *Europa en Amerika, of de toekomstige betrekkingen der beschaafde wereld.* Door Dr. C. F. von Schmidt-Phiseldek. In het Nederduitsch vertaald, door T. Olivier-Schilperoort. Amsterdam, 1820, XII, 284 pp

Swedish: *Europa och America, eller den civiliserade verldens framtida tillstånd, i perspektiv,* af C. F. Schmidt-Phiseldeck. Stockholm, 1821, VIII, 262 pp

An American translation was said by Alexander Hill Everettt to have been published. He wrote: 'I observe with pleasure that a translation of this eloquent and philosophical work has been published in the United States'.* It has not been possible to verify this and the translation is not noted by *The American Quarterly Review's* reviewer (see review listed below, p 413).

Reviews

Danish: [A. C. Gierlew] in *Dansk Litteratur-Tidende,* 1820, No. 36, pp 561–73; No. 37, pp 577–92; No. 38, pp 593–608; No. 39, pp 609–24; No. 40, pp 625–40, *cf.* the author's 'Bemærkninger i Anledning af den i Litteratur-Tidende for 1820 indførte Recensi-on' [Remarks concerning the review in the *Litteratur-Tidende* for 1820] *loc. cit.,* pp 653–56, and 'Anmelderens Svar' [the reviewer's reply], *loc.cit.,* pp 685–88. *Nyeste Skilderie af Kjøbenhavn,* Vol. 33, 1820, No. 70, pp 1109–16; No. 71, pp 1123–29. C. N. David in *Maanedsskrift for Litteratur,* 1832, VIII, pp 136–57 [review of the 1832 version].

German: *Leipziger Literatur-Zeitung,* 1820, II, No. 181, pp 1445–48. *Allgemeine Literatur-Zeitung,* 1820, III, No. 280, pp 490–94. K. F. Carstens in *Heidelbergische Jahrbücher der Literatur,* 1820, No. 28, pp 440–48; No. 29, pp 449–52.

French: P. A. Heiberg in *Revue Encyclopédique,* VII, 1820, pp 570–71.

American: *American Quarterly Review,* 9, 1831, pp 398–419.

Swedish: *Courieren från Stockholm,* 1821, No. 41, pp 169–74; No. 42, pp 177–79. *Stockholms Posten,* 1821, No. 170 [4 pp].

---

* EVERETT, A. H., *Europe: Or a General Survey of the Present Situation of the Principal Powers with Conjectures.* Boston, 1822, p 433, note.

Other mention in contemporary literature

EVERETT, A. H., *Europe: Or a General Survey of the Present Situation of the Principal Powers with Conjectures.* Boston 1822, pp 432–36.
EVERETT, A. H., *America: or a General Survey of the Political Situation of the Several Powers of the Western Continent, with Conjectures on their Future Prospects.* Philadelphia, 1827, pp 68–69.
TROLLOPE, F., *Domestic Manners of the Americans.* London, 1927 (1832), pp 280–81.

Notes to 'Europe and America'

Information about persons and places mentioned in Schmidt-Phiseldeck's book has not been included in the Notes but is given briefly in the Index. For ease of reference, some subjects have been cross-referenced between Index and Notes.

It has not been possible to correct misprints in the photographic reprint of *Europe and America*. Some corrections have been made in the Notes, but only in so far as the sense is affected. See also p [258].

p 3: peace of Ghent; between USA and Great Britain. Ended the war of 1812–14 without cession of territory.

Attack of the British; the British frigate *Leopard* attacked the *Chesapeake* off Norfolk Roads on 22 June 1807 (not 20 July 1807).

p 5: The revolution; the Spanish revolt against France in 1808, the year in which France had deposed the Bourbons from the Spanish throne in favor of Napoleon's brother, Joseph Bonaparte.

p 9: peace of Westphalia; 1648. Ended the Thirty Years War of 1618–48. Often regarded as beginning of modern history of Europe.

p 13: edict of Nantes; 1598. The Edict of Nantes guaranteed Protestant rights in France. It was revoked in 1685.

p 14: celebrated treaty; concluded 1703 (not 1702).

p 15: since 1735; Sicily and the Kingdom of Naples were united under the Spanish Bourbons from 1735.

Ambassade au Thibet; English title: *An Account of an Embassy to the Court of the Teshoo Lama in Tibet; containing a Narrative of a Journey through Bootan, and part of Tibet.* London, 1800.

279

p 16: disturbances at Geneva; 1762–68, 1782 and from 1790 (in connection with the French Revolution).

p 26: Essai politique & c; in several editions. Schmidt-Phiseldeck used *Essai politique sur le royaume de la Nouvelle-Espagne.* Tome 1–5. Paris, 1811. 8°.

p 34: government of the Terrorists; (la Terreur), period of the French Revolution (Sept. 1793–July 1794), during which some 42,000 people were guillotined.

p 37: peace of Campo Formio; 17 Oct. 1797, between France (Bonaparte) and Austria. Ended the war in Italy (1796–97).
treaties of Basel; Basle, 5 April 1795, peace between France and Prussia; 22 July 1795, peace between France and Spain.
18th of Fructidor; name given to a French Republican *coup d'état* which took place on 18 Fructidor, Year V, *i.e.* 4 Sept. 1797 (not 5 Sept.). The coup was carried out with troops sent to France from Italy by Bonaparte, paving his way to power.

p 38: negotiations in Rastadt; 9 Dec. 1797–23 April 1799. The conference was held under the terms of the peace of Campo Formio. In negotiations between France, Austria, Prussia and a number of smaller countries an unsuccessful attempt was made to achieve agreement on the future of Germany.

p 51: York's celebrated convention; Yorck (not York), commander-in-chief of Napoleon's Prussian auxiliaries in the Russian campaign (1812), concluded an agreement with the Russians for the temporary neutrality of his troops during the retreat from Moscow. This, made without the authority of the King of Prussia, set off the Prussian revolt against Napoleon.

p 53: Treaty of Reichenbach the 15th June 1813; guaranteed British aid to Russia and Prussia for continuing the war against Napoleon.
Congress at Prague; held June-August 1813; between France and the four allied Great Powers, Britain, Prussia, France and Austria. Napoleon was unwilling to make concessions, only wanting to gain time. The congress ended without result on 10 August. The next day, Austria declared war on France.
the decisive battle of Leipsic; 16–19 Oct. 1813; France was defeated by Austria, Prussia and Russia.

p 54: a congress had been opened at Chatillon; on 5 Feb.–19 March 1814 Châtillon-sur-Seine was the scene of unsuccessful peace negotiations between Napoleon and the Allies.

p 68: the defeats at Austerlitz and Friedland; at Austerlitz in 1805 France defeated Austria and Russia; at Friedland in 1807 France defeated Russia.

p 70: constitutional Charter; the *Charte constitutionnelle,* granted by Louis XVIII on 4 June 1814, was the French Constitution until 1830.

p 73: Holy Alliance; it was signed in Paris on 26 Sept. 1815 (not 15 Sept. 1815).

p 81: Oddy; i.e. William Playfair. The book's full title is: *European Commerce, shewing new channels of trade with the continent of Europe: detailing the produce of Russia, Prussia, Sweden, Denmark, and Germay; with a view of the trade of the Kingdom of Great Britain and Ireland. Illustrated with a canal and river map of Europe.* London, 1805. The quoted information is from Book VI, Chapter X.

p 87: formal treaties; in 1818 a convention was concluded between Freiburg and Portugal (to which Brazil was subject), enabling Swiss citizens from Freiburg to found, on favorable terms, a colony, Novo Friburgo, north of Rio de Janeiro. The colony was not a success and had disappeared by about 1840.

p 88: Gagern's work; the reference is to FÜRSTENWRÖTHER, M. v., *Der Deutsche in Nord-Amerika* (edited with an introduction by H. C. E. von Gagern). Stuttgart and Tübingen, 1818.

p 98: or much less amongst; read: *not to speak of.*

p 99: Humboldt, Essai politique I. p. 304; see note to p 26.

p 113: Essai politique Tome IV. pag. 259; see note to p 26.

p 114: latest description; FISCHER, C.-A., *Neuestes Gemälde von Brasilien.* 2 V. Leipzig, 1819.

p 117: the latter unfortunate Mahratta prince; Daulot Rão Sind(h)ia. In 1818, after several years of fighting the British, he became their client.

minor warfare of the Seiks and Pindharris; after 1803–04, when the Mahrattā Confederation, with which the Pindaris were associated, had been broken up, the Pindaris carried out raids independently against British territory. The Pindari War

(1817–18) put a stop to these. The Sikhs remained a threat to the British down to the end of the Second Sikh War (1849). *William Playfair's calculations;* they occur in *Strictures on the Asiatic Establishments of Great Britain; with a view to an enquiry into the true interests of the East India Company.* London, 1799.

p 118: The lasting Duration of such an organization; the British East India Company, originally a trading monopoly, was involved from the middle of the eighteenth century in politics as an agent of British imperialism in India.

p 119: transatlantic; read: *transoceanic.*

Fullarton's celebrated work; i.e. *A view of the English Interest in India, and an account of the Military operations in the Southern parts of the Peninsula during the campaigns of 1782–84. In two letters.* London, 1787.

p 125: Humboldt makes mention; vide: *Essai politique sur le royaume de la Nouvelle-Espagne,* 2. Paris, 1811, pp 10–24.

p. 147: Political Journal; i.e. *Politisches Journal.* Hamburg.

p 163: In states; e.g. Denmark-Norway, 1813.

p 197: the latest work of Mr. von Humboldt; i.e. *Voyage aux régions équinoxiales du nouveau Continent fait en 1799, 1800, 1801, 1802, 1803 et 1804, par Al. de Humboldt et A. Bonpland.* Première Partie. Relation Historique. Tome Second. Paris, 1819. The quoted information is on pp 35–37 and p 122.

p 205: By these means ... of itself bring about; read: *By these means – and we particularly request that this may not be lost sight of – that would take place voluntarily, according to the choice and dispositions of those to whom the direction of these objects is entrusted, which will otherwise shortly in any case be brought about by necessity.*

p 214: idea of an Areopagus; an allusion to the Holy Alliance, which Schmidt-Phiseldeck rated highly (*cf.* Postcript).

p 229: The preparatory; from *Kritik der Urteilskraft.* Berlin/Libau, 1790, pp 258–260; English edition: *The Critique of Judgement.* Oxford, 1952, pp 226–27.

282

Notes on the Plates

In the Notes the text on each individual plate (portraits excepted) usually consists of four elements.
The first is a brief excerpt from the text of the original book; the second is the subtitle of the plate; the third is an explanatory note, where called for; the fourth gives the bibliography of the plate.

Plates between p 12 and p 13:

Conrad Georg Friedrich Elias von Schmidt-Phiseldeck (1770–1832).

Unsigned and undated painting, according to family tradition painted posthumously by the Danish artist Wilhelm Marstrand (1810–73).
Privately owned. Copenhagen.

The price of labor has been reduced much below the limits, which would enable the labourer himself or a family, to enjoy a species of prosperity. *See* p 76.

Norwegian iron works c. 1790.

In Norway, in the 1780s and 1790s, poor living standards and low wages caused unrest among the workers of several copper and iron works in Southern Norway as at the Bærum Iron Works, shown above, west of Oslo.

Undated aquatint from a painted original by the
Dane Christian August Lorentzen (1746–1828).
The Royal Collection of Prints, Copenhagen.

Plates between p 16 and p 17:

Alexander Hill Everett (1790–1847). American diplomat and
editor of the periodical *The North American Review*. When
Everett in 1822 analysed the political and social conditions in
the major European countries he showed firsthand knowledge of Schmidt-Phiseldeck's book. While the two authors were
in agreement on the potential power position of America,
Everett however saw 'no reason to anticipate that the emancipation of the whole of America will have a less favourable
effect upon Europe in general, than that which was produced
upon the prosperity of England, by the independence of the
United States.'

Miniature painting c. 1830–c. 1835 by the American
Washington Blanchard (active c. 1830–c. 1849).

Reproduced from The New-York Historical Society, ed., *Ca-
talogue of American Portraits in the New-York Historical Society.*
I–II. New Haven & London, 1974. I, No. 651, p 258.

The quotation is from Everett's book, *Europe: Or a General
Survey of the Present Situation of the Principal Powers with Conjectures.* Boston, 1822, p 434.

The industry of the diligent inhabitants of the British Islands
is principally founded on their coal mines. *See* p 17.

'The Coal Waggon'.

Lithograph 1821 by the French painter Théodore Géricault
(1791–1824), done during a visit to England 1820–22.
The Royal Collection of Prints, Copenhagen.

Plates between p 22 and p 23:

In the West-India islands the growth of plantations is likely ever to remain the principal object. *See* p 108.

Sugar plantation on the Island of St. Croix in the West Indies.

Coloured drawing by the Danish naval officer Frederik von Scholten (1796–1853). The drawing, dated August 1833, shows the plantation 'Castle Coakley'.
The Danish Maritime Museum at Kronborg Castle, Elsinore.

The United states, are in the habit of sending annually a considerable number of vessels, to East India ports, from Salem, Boston, New York, Philadelphia, Charleston &c. *See* p 119 f.

Port and city of Philadephia.

Engraving in JANSON, Charles William, *The Stranger in America: Containing Observations made during a long Residence in that Country, on the Genius, Manners and Customs of the People of the United States.* London, 1807.
From a drawing by an unknown artist under the supervision of the author. Frontispiece. Dated 1807.

In the Danish-State, the industry of the inhabitants, characterized the latter period of the eighteenth century. *See* p 21.

Langelinie. Port of Copenhagen 1794.

Since the 1730s the Danish capital was the point of departure for annually recurring commercial expeditions to China. Not least during the American War of Independence (1776–83) and the French Revolutionary Wars of the 1790s did the Chinese trade mean substantial gains for enterprising Co-

penhagen merchants. Ships would primarily carry back tea
but also porcelain and silk. Silver was used almost exclusively
as a means of payment. Seen here is the outfitting of a China-
man. In the background are units of the Danish and Swedish
navies.

Coloured drawing by the Danish painter Terkild Emanuel
Lønning (1762–1823) entitled 'Danish and Swedish Squad-
rons Riding at Anchor in the Roads of Copenhagen in the
Year MDCCXCIV'.
The Danish Maritime Museum at Kronborg Castle, Elsinore.

The power of the elements, in alliance with the just cause,
assisted in annihilating an army, which had not had its equal in
the annals of European warfare. *See* p 50.

Napoleon's retreat from Moscow 1812.
'Boney Hatching a Bulletin or Snug Winter Quarters!!!'

Engraving by the Englishman George Cruikshank (1792–
1878). Printed in *Cobbett's Political Register*, ed., William Cobbett, London, December 5, 1812.

Reproduced from GEORGE, M. Dorothy, *English Political
Caricature 1793–1832. A Study of Opinion and Propaganda.* I–II.
Oxford University Press, Oxford, 1959. II. Plate 53.

The text reads:
Officer: Vat de devil shall Ve say in de Bulletin?
Napoleon: Say!!!! why Say We have got into Comfortable
Winter Quarters and the Weather is very fine & will last 8 days
longer. Say we have got plenty of Soup Meagre, plenty of
Minced meat – Grilld Bears fine Eating – driveing Cut – us –
off to the Devil. Say we shall be at home at Xmas to dinner –
give my love to darling – don't let John Bull Know that I have
been Cowpoxed – tell a good lie about the Cossacks. D – e it tell
any thing but the Truth.

Plates between p 66 and p 67:

The first instance of an European kingdom, being dependant upon an American main state. *See* p 66.

King Juan VI of Portugal and Brazil and his entourage in the vicinity of Rio de Janeiro, c. 1820.

The ruler of Portugal remained in Brazil from 1807 to 1821.

Lithograph in HENDERSON, James, *A History of the Brazil; Comprising its Geography, Commerce, Colonization, Aboriginal Inhabitants, & & &*. London, 1821.
From a drawing by the author. Frontispiece. Undated.

But what sacrifices did this not cost the people! Since the popular migrations of the ancient tribes, there has never been seen such distress and misery, as have reigned in the later times. *See* p 69.

'The Disaters of War'.

Etching by Francisco de Goya (1746–1828), reproduced from *Los Desastres de la Guerra: Coleccion de ochenta láminas inventadas y grabadas al agua fuerte por Don Francisco Goya*. Publicada de Rl. Academia de Nobles Artes de San Fernando. Madrid, 1863. No. 26, designated 'No se puede mirar' ['One can't look']. The Royal Collection of Prints, Copenhagen.

Plates between p 82 and p 83:

Inanimate powers are being daily substituted more and more, in the place of human hands, by reason of the rapid progress the mechanical arts have made. *See* p 81.

The rapid progress of the mechanical arts.

In England the manufacture of cotton cloth was characterized by its relatively high degree of mechanisation; thus the first power loom was introduced in 1786. It was powered by horses, water or steam. The technological advances generated substantial opposition among cotton industry workers. For the handloom weavers mechanisation would often mean unemployment while the factory workers felt completely at the mercy of the entrepreneurs.

The picture shows how hydraulic power was ingeniously exploited to power all machines in the cotton mill of the Strutt family at Belper, Derbyshire, 'one of the most complete cotton mills, we have ever visited'.

Engraving in REES, Abraham, *The Cyclopædia; or Universal Dictionary of Arts, Sciences, and Literature. Plates.* Vol II. Cotton Manufacture. Plate XIV, Figs. 2 and 3, London, 1820.
From a drawing by the Englishman John Farey Junior (1791–1851). Undated.

The quotation is from *op. cit.,* Vol. XXII, London, 1819. *See* 'Manufacture of Cotton'.

The spoils of the new world first occasioned the present extensive use of jewels. *See* p 95.

Negroes washing for diamonds in Brazil.

The exploitation of the Brazilian diamond deposits, discovered in the 1720s, was since 1771 under the direct control of the Portuguese Crown. The washing was done by black slaves who were closely watched by white supervisors to prevent smuggling. The precautionary measures were inadequate, however.

Engraving in MAWE, John, *Travels in the Interior of Brazil, Particularly in the Gold and Diamond Districts of that fine Country; Describing the Population, Manners, and Customs of the Inhabitants, the Climate, Natural Productions, Agriculture and Commerce; also, the Method of working their Mines.* London, 1815.
From a drawing by the author. Frontispiece. Dated 1812.

Plates between p 98 and p 99:

The ox is found every where at present, either as a domestic animal, affording nourishment, or in a state of nature. *See* p 98.

Ox hunting in Brazil, north of Rio de Janeiro.

Engraving in WIED-NEUWIED, Maximilian Prinz, *Reise nach Brasilien in den Jahren 1815 bis 1817*. I-II. Frankfurt a. M., 1820–21.
From a drawing by the author, processed by the signature of G. Opitz who is probably identical with the Austrian George Emanuel Opitz (1775–1841). II, at p 197. Undated.

For hitherto, the most European goods, can be imported cheaper from across the Atlantic, than if fabricated on the spot. The American government, has notwithstanding acted here very wisely, in having let the thing take its natural course, which first allows fabrics and manufactories to flourish, when capital can no longer be placed more advantageously in land, when the raw productions are at hand, and as cheap, as in other foreign rival states. *See* p 106 f.

Barclay's Iron Works at Saugerties on the Hudson River, United States.

The rich coal and iron deposits in Pennsylvania and New York were prerequisite to the establisment of iron works such as Barclay's at Saugerties in the State of New York.

Engraving in HINTON, John Howard, ed., *The History and Topography of the United States*. I-II, 2. ed., London, 1834.
From a drawing by the Irish-born painter William Guy Wall (1792–died after 1864). II, at p 93. Dated 1831.

Plates between p 126 and p 127:

The cities of South, rather than of North America, are embellished with monuments of the plastic arts, which may serve to
inspire future genius. *See* p 125.

Buenos Aires.

Unsigned and undated engraving in AZARA, Félix de, *Voy-
ages dans l'Amérique méridionale depuis 1781 jusqu'en 1801. Collection de Planches.* Paris, 1809. Planche No. XVII.

Internal and external communication of which in many parts
of Europe, the outlines only exist, are no where arrived at
perfection, except perhaps in England. *See* p 142.

The Bridgewater Canal between Worsley and Manchester in
England.

In the decades around the year 1800 one of the main arteries
of the English canal network was the Bridgewater Canal between Worsley and Manchester, which was built between 1759
and 1764. This link reduced the price of coal in Manchester
considerably and thus became an essential factor in the development of industrial production in the area. The construction of Barton Bridge (shown in picture), which leads the
canal across the river Irwell, was considered an unusual feat in
its day.

Engraving in AIKIN, J., *A Description of the Country from Thirty
to Forty Miles round Manchester.* London, 1795. From a drawing
by the Dutchman Jan Swertner (1746–1813). Plate 10, at
p 113. Dated 1794.

290

Plates between p 206 and p 207:

It has been looked upon as an advantage in our improved public shools, that boys of very different ranks of life, pass them in joint emulation in one common course of instruction and amusements. *See* p 205.

Mutual instruction in a Danish school.

The so-called mutual or Lancasterian educational system, developed by the Englishman Joseph Lancaster, was introduced into Danish schools in the post-Napoleonic era at the prompting of King Frederik VI. The system was founded on the concept that any boy who can read, can teach and that hence a substantial part of the teaching can be handled by the more experienced students. As shown in the picture, one of the tasks of such students or monitors was to correct orthographic or calliographic mistakes in front of everybody else. Military precision and precedence were principal features of the system.

Unsigned and undated lithograph in BRUUN, Jens Worm, *Den Lancasterske Skoleindretnings Historie* [History of the Lancasterian School System]. Copenhagen, 1820. Tab. I, Fig. II.

The servitude and slavish dependence, in which the acquirement of their daily bread, and the struggle after physical existence, have hitherto chained the majority of the mass of people will become less frequent. *See* p 217 .

Manpower in a Danish cloth mill.

During the last years of the Napoleonic Wars the government-owned Military Cloth Mill at Usserød north of Copenhagen employed around 160 children most of whom were orphans. Conditions both at and off the place of work seem to have been objectionable, here as well as elsewhere. At the initiative of individual entreprenuers efforts were made to remedy the most blatant injustices, but not until the early 1870s was it realised that the legislature must take regulatory action.

The picture shows a carding machine. The worker at left operates the machine by turning the handle while the boy in back of him places the raw wool on the feed rollers.

Unsigned painting on a wooden plate for cloth manufacturer Johan Gottlieb Cramer, presented on July 12, 1815.
The Royal Copenhagen Rifle Society, Copenhagen.

Plates between p 208 and p 209:

Northern and even American mariners have engrossed the navigation of the Spanish peninsula in the Mediterranean, at the entrance of which, nature seems to have placed it as a guardian. *See* p 130.

The American frigate *Ontario* anchored off the city of Smyrna (Izmir) on the Turkish Mediterranean coast, 1825.

Coloured drawing by the Danish naval officer Frederik von Scholten (1796–1853). Dated 1825.
The Danish Maritime Museum at Kronborg Castle, Elsinore.

Does not the kingdom of the Osmans, from the limits of Hungary and Transylvania to the shores of Asia Minor, form a part of European soil? Have not its cities and villages, its monuments of ancient art and science, been built and founded by the most chosen of the European nations? *See* p 144.

The Acropolis of Athens.

A foreign element in an European framework. In front of the Acropolis stands a Turkish cemetary.

Lithograph by the Frenchman Louis Dupré (1789–1837) in

his *Voyage à Athènes et à Constantinople ou Collection de Portraits, de Vues et de Costumes grecs et ottomans.* Paris, 1825. Planche XXIII.
From at sketch made during a stay in Greece in 1819.

The well-mounted Cumanches. *See* p 246.

'Comanche Chasing Buffalo With Bows and Lances'.

Painting from 1834 by the American painter George Catlin (1796–1872).
Smithsonian Institution, Washington D.C.

Plates between p 222 and p 223:

In order to attain a state of prosperity, no quicker resource presents itself, than that of commerce; hence the mercantile spirit, which certainly is predominant in America. *See* p 222.

South Street in New York City, United States.

Undated engraving from an aquatint, probably done in 1828 by the English-born painter William James Bennett (c. 1787–1844), entitled 'South St. from Maiden Lane'.
The I. N. Phelps Stokes Collection of American Historical Prints. Prints Division, The New York Public Library, New York.

The proficiency in oratory, which the public character and the discussions of the legislative senates have rendered peculiarly the province of the American, is likely to emerge from that profusion of declamatory phraseology, which at present generally stamps it. *See* p 230 f.

Harvard College, Cambridge, Mass., United States.

Rhetoric and oratory were prominent subjects at Harvard College from the beginning of the 19th century.

Engraving in HINTON, John Howard, ed., *The History and Topography of the United States*. I-II, 2. ed., London, 1834.
From a drawing by the American artist Alexander Jackson Davis (1803–92). II, at p 470. Dated 1830.

Plate at the back of the book:

The great rivers and lakes of America profusely offer the means of an inland communication, which renders uncommon facilities to the rapid circulation of every production of industry and nature from the remotest parts. *See* p 108.

Opening of the Grand Erie Canal, United States.

The Grand Erie Canal connects Lake Erie with the Hudson River and the Atlantic, opening up the West. On the completion of the Canal in 1825 the Corporation of the City of New York arranged an aquatic procession from the lake to the Atlantic; assisted by the Navy the fleet is seen preparing to form in line at Brooklyn.

Undated lithograph by the French-born draftsman and painter Antoine Imbert (died c. 1835) in COLDEN, Cadwallader D., *Memoir, Prepared at the Request of a Committee of the Common Council of the City of New York and Presented to the Mayor of the City, at the Celebration of the Completion of the New York Canals. Appendix, Containing an Account of the Commemoration of the Completion of the Erie Canal by the Corporation of the City of New York. By Order of the Common Council*. New York, 1826, entitled 'The Fleet Preparing to form in Line'. At p 47.

The copy of the book used bears a dedication to the Danish Minister for Foreign Affairs Ernst Schimmelmann (1747–1831) from the City of New York, 1827.
The Royal Library, Copenhagen.

Index

The Index comprises *Europe and America*, the *Postscript* and the *Notes to 'Europe and America'* but not the *Notes on the Plates*.

All names of places and persons have been included, except 'Europe', 'America' and 'Schmidt-Phiseldeck', and names in book titles and imprints.

300

patriot, 5–6, 124

Mississippi, 220

Molucca Islands, 111

Monterey (town in Mexico), 116

Montevideo (city in Uruguay), 246

More, Thomas (1477–1535), English humanist and statesman; author of *Utopia*, 1516, 270

Morea. *See* Peloponnese

Moreau, Jean Victor (1763–1813), French general, 36, 49

Moscow, 50, 251, 279

Murat Joachim (1767–1815), marshal of France, king of Naples as Joachim Napoleon 1808–15, 63, 74

Møller, Jens (1779–1833), Danish author and professor, 269

N

Nantes (French city), 13, 278. *See* note to p 13

Naples (city), 38, 74

Naples (kingdom, comprised southern Italy), 278

Napoleon Bonaparte (1769–1821), emperor of France 1804–14/15, 35–36, 38–39, 41, 44, 47, 49, 51, 53–56, 60–64, 67, 74, 141, 278–80

National Bank (of Denmark), 262

Netherlands (including present-day Belgium 1814–1830/31), 16, 34, 60, 62, 64, 71, 76, 123, 191

Neuchâtel (Swiss canton), 63

Neva (Russian river); in its delta St Petersburg, founded 1703, 68

New Biscay (*i.e.* Chihuahua, Mexico), 246

New Hampshire, 238

New Holland (historical name for part of Australia), 123

New Jersey, 238

New South Wales (Australia), 256

New Spain, Viceroyalty of (1535–1821), included Mexico, the Carribean Islands, Central America north of Panama, and the coast of Venezuela, 99, 101

New Vevay, Swiss colony on the Ohio river. Founded 1804 with governmental aid to promote the cultivation of the wine, 99

New York, 120, 238

Nicomedia (city of north-western Aisa Minor), 148

Nile, 40

Norfolk Roads (Virginia), 278

North America. *See* United States

North American Union. *See*